Praise for Literary Agents

"Full of good, sound advice."
—Michael Korda, best-selling author and Seni...

"So chock-full of delicious, wise, witty, and often laugh-out-loud quotes about the writer's life, the editor's life, the agent's life, that there's no way attention can flag. It's absolutely the last word on literary agents, and the most humorous."
—Richard Curtis, AAR, Richard Curtis Associates

"A most impressive job. . . . There's more information here than I ever thought existed. It's so thorough, it seems almost encyclopedic."
—Albert Zuckerman, AAR, Writers House

"I don't think a writer has to read any other book to understand the entire publishing business fully and write successfully. It's fun and packed with information."
—Andrea Brown, AAR, Andrea Brown Literary Agency

"Michael Larsen's book should be required reading for all authors—published and unpublished."
—Patricia Teal, AAR, Patricia Teal Agency

"A great job."
—Susan Ann Protter, AAR, Literary Agent

"First-rate. Lots of useful nitty-gritty information and enough inspiration so all the realism isn't too discouraging."
—Peter Ginna, Senior Editor, Crown Publishing Group

"Where was this book twenty years ago when I began my business? If I could have read this book, I may have decided to become an astronaut instead—it would have been easier."
—Sandra Watt, Sandra Watt Associates

"This book is bright, funny, informative, and well paced—an illuminating insider's look into the world of literary agents. I wouldn't be surprised if booksellers started charging customers a 15 percent fee just to browse through it."
—Jonathan Karp, Editor, Random House

"Smart, savvy, irresistibly upbeat. Your best guide through the jungle of publishing. Even more helpful than the original edition, which many writers found indispensable."

–*Arthur Orrmont, Author Aid Associates, and Co-editor,* Literary Agents of North America *(5th Ed.)*

"Even after sixteen years in publishing, seven of them as an agent, I am always learning—and often teaching. I'll recommend *Literary Agents.* I read it saying, 'Yes, yes, yes.'"

–*Sheree Bykofsky, AAR, Sheree Bykofsky Associates*

"Simply splendid from beginning to end, and a book which I will recommend to every author who crosses my path. Its wit and wisdom and enthusiasm are so persuasive, it make me want to sit right down and write a book—but I will take an aspirin and lie down until the feeling passes! A fine contribution for writers, publishers, and agents alike. It made me laugh out loud with its rare ability to combine humor with good, solid information."

–*Rosalie Heacock, Heacock Literary Agency*

"The best book for writers on marketing their work just got better. This is *the* book I recommend at writers conferences. What a boon to have it available again, and in an updated, expanded version."

–*Jane Jordan Browne, Literary Agent, Multimedia Product Development*

"It is always great to see a book from a real pro . . . and in one volume hear a voice that speaks to those on the search to get published and for us already in the business to learn a great deal. A real service to us all."

–*Michael Hamilburg, Mitchell J. Hamilburg Agency*

"A great piece of work."

–*Neil Olson, AAR, Donadio & Ashworth Literary Representatives*

"A valuable resource for the beginning writer."

–*Arnold Goodman, AAR, Goodman Associates*

"An absolutely vital tool for writers. It gives them a big head start in today's competitive market."

–*Marcia Amsterdam, Marcia Amsterdam Agency*

Literary Agents

Wiley Books for Writers Series

Book Editors Talk to Writers, by Judy Mandell

Magazine Editors Talk to Writers, by Judy Mandell

The Elements of Storytelling: How to Write Compelling Fiction,
by Peter Rubie

Networking at Writer's Conferences: From Contacts to Contracts,
by Steven D. Spratt and Lee G. Spratt

Other Books by Michael Larsen

How to Write a Book Proposal

The Worry Bead Book: The World's Oldest and Simplest Way to Beat Stress

With Hal Zina Bennett

How to Write with a Collaborator

With Elizabeth Pomada

California Publicity Outlets (now called Metro California Media)

Painted Ladies: San Francisco's Resplendent Victorians

Daughters of Painted Ladies: America's Resplendent Victorians

The Painted Ladies Revisited: San Francisco's Resplendent Victorians Inside
and Out

How to Create Your Own Painted Lady: A Comprehensive Guide to
Beautifying Your Victorian Home

The Painted Ladies Guide to Victorian California

America's Painted Ladies: The Ultimate Celebration of Our Victorians

The Painted Ladies Calendar

Literary Agents

What They Do, How They Do It, and How to Find and Work with the Right One for You

REVISED AND EXPANDED

Michael Larsen, AAR

John Wiley & Sons, Inc.

New York • Chichester • Brisbane • Toronto • Singapore

Library of Congress Cataloging-in-Publication Data

Larsen, Michael.
    Literary agents : what they do, how they do it, and how to find and work with the right one for you / by Michael Larsen. — Revised and expanded.
      p. cm.
    Includes bibliographical references.
    ISBN 0-471-13046-X (pbk. : alk. paper)
    1. Literary agents. I. Title.
PN163.L37 1996
070.5'2—dc20   95-53093

Printed in the United States of America

10 9 8 7 6 5 4 3 2 1

To the writers this book inspires to do their best work and show
an affirming flame, and to Elizabeth, my divine commission

Contents

9 Following the Money: What an Agent Does after the Sale

10 Hooked on Books: A Terrific Day in the Life of an Agent

11 Terminal Transgressions: What to Do When the Honeymoon Is Over

Forewarning

This book is directed to writers working on book-length adult fiction and nonfiction. In its tone and approach, it's a very California book. It looks at agents holistically (what could be more California?) in the context of understanding writing, the changing world of books, and yourself. Understanding the agenting and publishing process will help lessen the unavoidable anxieties that authors endure.

This book was also written to help you earn the compensation and position in the literary community that you and your work deserve by showing you the fastest way to obtain the agent, publisher, and deal you want for your book.

While writing, I tried to imagine you as one of the many writers my partner and I speak to year after year who are intimidated by agents and publishing. The book has seven goals:

- To change your life by changing the way you think about publishing, writing, and perhaps yourself

- To convince you that if you have enough talent and persistence, you will get an agent and your books will be published

- To present the trends and realities of writing, publishing, and agenting, which you need to know to get your books published

- To encourage you to create a network with other professionals in the book community, especially writers who share your goals and problems and with whom you may be able to forge enduring personal and professional friendships. Writing may be a lonely calling, but even if you live in the middle of nowhere, it doesn't have to be a solitary enterprise.

- To be an informative, enjoyable, and inspiring reading experience for writers, publishers, and agents

- To be enough of a service to agents that they will say, "This is what I've always wanted to tell my writers."

- To create a dialogue about your needs, problems, questions, suggestions, and experiences that can be used to improve the next edition of this book. I have learned much from writers and want to learn more. If you, too, would like the next edition to be better, please send me your ideas. Many thanks in advance.

When writers talk to one another, they may discover that they have had very different experiences with the same agent, editor, or publisher. Every relationship has its own dynamics, depending on the personalities involved, the fate of the book, and the moment. The relationship will probably change as the project progresses.

The phenomenon is part of the reason why writing this book was the hardest, most intimidating job of my life. To generalize with complete accuracy about three endeavors that are as personal, complex, and varied as writing, publishing, and agenting is impossible. No one has a monopoly on truth or virtue. Only the past is certain, and even then, people disagree about it. The only absolute truth is what works for you.

Because books are catalysts for personal and social change, the freedom to write and publish them is essential to our well-being as individuals and as a nation. I wanted every word of this book to sing because I want it to transform your life. However, if all it does is help you appreciate the value of books and the effort that goes into writing, selling, and publishing them, the effort will have been worthwhile.

Acknowledgments for the First Edition

Many generous people are entitled to share the credit for this book. The first person who must be thanked is Carol Cartaino, former editor in chief at Writer's Digest Books, who dared to tempt fate by asking a partner in a small San Francisco literary agency to write a book.

As with *How to Write a Book Proposal*, the staff at Writer's Digest Books—editor Barbara O'Brien, Howard Wells, John Andraud, and Jo Hoff—has been professional and a pleasure to work with.

To Dominick Abel, Georges Borchardt, Knox Burger, Diane Cleaver, John Cushman, Kris Dahl, Anita Diamant, Sandy Dijkstra, Peter Fleming, Barthold Fles, Joyce Frommer, Russ Galen, Tom Hart, Owen Laster, Ned Leavitt, Scott Meredith, Henry Morrison, Marvin Moss, Gil Parker, Susan Protter, Roberta Pryer, Charlotte Sheedy, Peter Shepherd, Bobbe Siegel, Phil Spitzer, and Al Zuckerman, who took the time to share their wisdom about the business of agenting with me, I am extremely grateful.

For their views from abroad, I would like to thank the following foreign agents: Eliane Benisti, David Grossman, Ib Lauritzen, Ruth Liepman, William Miller, Elfrieda Pexa, and Jonathan Webber.

Special thanks to editors Bob Bender, Liz Hock, and Ann La Farge, author Bill Paxson, Suzanne Juergensen, and those agents who read part or all of the manuscript and whose comments have been incorporated into the final version: Marcia Amsterdam, Rick Balkin, Jim and Rosalie Heacock, Perry Knowlton, and Arthur Orrmont.

By going over parts of the manuscript word by word, my agent, Peter Skolnik, improved the book a great deal. His knowledge, authority, and sensitivity inspire both affection and respect.

Thanks go to Bobbe Siegel for permission to use her agency contract and for the friendship so warmly extended by her and her husband, Dick.

By joining the index party, thanks to three fine friends and innocent bystanders: Alberta Cooper, Toni Anderson, and Bill Cox.

Over the years, many publishing professionals—editors, for the most part—have shared their insights with my partner, Elizabeth Pomada, and me. Among them are John Baker, Bob Bender, Cornelia and Mike Bessie, Toni Burbank, Adene Corns, John Dodds, Joyce Engelson, Joe Esposito, Larry Freundlich, Ash Green, Pat Holt, Jane Isay, Betty Jurus, Joe Kanon, Michael Korda, Jim Landis, Dick Marek, Helen Myer, Brad and Sydny Miner, Luther Nichols, Andy Ross, Jon Segel, and Bob Wyatt. To all of you, named and unnamed, our thanks.

Elizabeth and I would not have gotten as far as we have without the trust and faith of our clients. Thank you for giving us a chance, especially those of you responsible for my "terrific day."

This book evolved in part from the questions of students in our seminars and the participants at the writing classes, groups, and conferences where we've spoken. For giving us the chance to learn while we teach, thanks to the organizers of these events, especially Jon Kennedy and Steve and Meera Lester at the Writers Connection; and Paul Lazarus and Mary and Barnaby Conrad of the Santa Barbara Writer's Conference.

Thanks also to author Ron Lichty for allowing me to sit in on one of his excellent seminars on promotion for authors. Some of his ideas found their way into the section on promotion.

Kudos to Al Magary, Espon computer maven, whom I could always call when my QX-10 started acting up. The book wouldn't be as good as it is if my Epson hadn't made the manuscript so easy to revise.

As always, the advice, support, and encouragement of our families—Ray and Maryanne Larsen, Carol Larsen, Rita Pomada, and Sally Ross—have helped keep us going.

Nothing makes you appreciate how hard it is to write a good book as much as trying to write one. Having to put my knowledge in a book that will be judged by agents, editors, clients, and strangers who make their living reading between the lines made the task more onerous. At the same time, I feel very honored that fate chose me rather than one of my more experienced colleagues to write about the profession. I hope they believe that the book does them justice.

Writing this book has given me the chance to repay what agenting and publishing have done for me. Even more important is what I owe to the authors who got me hooked on books. Short of snuggling with Elizabeth, nothing beats a book I can't tear myself away from, especially if I can read it without the phone ringing!

Elizabeth Pomada got started in publishing and agenting before I did, and she has been with me from day one as agent, author, and partner. Without Elizabeth, I wouldn't have become an agent, and this book would not have been written. I hope that after reading the book, you feel that she chose the right path.

Acknowledgments for the Second Edition

My thanks to PJ Dempsey, who asked for a second edition, for her faith in the book, her patience with me, and her rigorous pencil. Many thanks also to Chris Jackson and Elaine O'Neal for their help, to copy editor Judith Mara Riotto for her excellent work, and to Jamie Temple at Pageworks.

To the writers around the country who have continued to write to me about the first edition, many thanks for your kind words. They helped convince me that a second edition was worth doing.

Sandwiched between my favorite jokes and quotes, the next *Book of Lists*, and a Sunday sermon is, I hope, the information you need about literary agents. My thanks to the cartoonists and the authors of the quotes in the book for their help in making the book more readable.

To Sam Horn, my thanks for reading the manuscript and for making many helpful suggestions. Many thanks to Antonia Anderson and Adele Horwitz for reviewing the manuscript three times.

Agents and editors always have bottomless piles to read. For stealing time from their appointed rounds to make many helpful suggestions, I am extremely grateful to editors Peter Gina and Jon Karp and to the following agents: Marcia Amsterdam, Andrea Brown, Jane Jordan Browne, Sheree Bykofsky, Martha Jane Casselman, Richard Curtis, the late Anita Diamant, Arnold Goodman, Mike Hamilburg, Rosalie Heacock, Neil Olson, Arthur Orrmont, Susan Ann Protter, Patricia Teal, Sandra Watt, and Albert Zuckerman. Their comments and encouragement were more valuable than they can know. Thanks to Andrea Brown also for her knowledge about children's books.

Thanks also to Rita Pomada for her comments about the first edition; Claudia Hagadus Long for her very helpful letter about the previous edition; and John Panza at R. R. Bowker.

Perry Knowlton, the retiring president of the Association of Authors'

Representatives, was kind enough to let me include the AAR's Code of Ethics. AAR legal counsel Ken Norwick greatly improved the chapter on agency agreements with his expertise.

For their insights about agenting and publishing here and abroad, my thanks to Chuck Adams, Patti Breitman, Martha Casselman, Sandra Dijkstra, David Grossman, Frances Halpern, Perry Knowlton, Michael Korda, Ruth Liepman, and William Miller.

To Mary and Barnaby Conrad of the Santa Barbara Writer's Conference, Steve and Meera Lester of the Writers Connection, Angela Smith of the Austin Writers League, and John Tullius of the Maui Writers Conference, our thanks for enabling us to learn as we teach.

Thanks again to our authors, whose faith in us enables us to earn a living and to continue to learn about the business.

Thanks to computer gurus Nic Grabien and Brian Carright for helping to keep my 286 working, and to Brian for retyping the book. For waking me with a smile and hot coffee, thanks to Lynnie Horrigan at The Morning Fix.

As in all things, our love and gratitude to our families for their love and support.

Last and most, my thanks to Elizabeth, who makes everything possible and whose help in reviewing the manuscript four times, keyboarding back and front matter, and being an encouraging helpmeet accounts a great deal for the manuscript being completed when it was and as well as it was.

Introduction: Read This Way

Three Approaches to Reading This Book

There was once a sign on a church announcing the next Sunday's sermon. The sign read

EVERLASTING PUNISHMENT
All Are Welcome.

I hope that you will find what follows more inspiring and pleasurable than punitive. This is the first interactive book about the world of publishing. You can choose between the following three ways to read it:

1. Reader's choice: Dip into the book anywhere, and just read what you want.

2. A logical choice: Read the book in the order in which it was written.
    You are reading this book because you need a literary agent, so the first two parts of the book are about agents. Part 1, "Hiring the Agent You Need," describes how agents work and how to find one. Part 2, "Understanding Your Agent," looks at what agents do and how to create and maintain a satisfactory relationship with yours. You may assume that the book has been structured in the most effective way.

3. The author's choice: Read Part 3 first, then read Parts 1 and 2. If you can stand the suspense, save the last chapter, "Writing High: The End of the Beginning," for last.
    What did the zen master say to the hot dog vendor? "Make me one with everything." Part 3 of the book, "How to Make Yourself Irresistible to Any Agent or Publisher," can't make you one with everything, but it will provide you with a perspective on writing,

publishing, and, most important of all, yourself. Part 3 is really a "prequel" to the rest of the book. Before you start looking for an agent, before you even start writing, you need an overview of the world you hope to enter.

Before you decide how you are going to read this book, ask yourself these questions:

- "Am I ready for an agent? Do I have a positive yet realistic perspective on the book business?" If not, chapter 13 will help you get started.

- "Is my ability to write strong enough to excite an agent?" If not, chapter 14 will help you understand how to develop your craft.

- "Do I have literary and financial goals, and am I fully committed to achieving them?" Chapter 15 will help you provide some of the information about yourself that agents will hope you have when you contact them.

Johnny Carson once confessed: "I was so naive as a kid I used to sneak behind the barn and do nothing." Writers contact us feeling defensive because they don't know anything about agenting or publishing, but part of an agent's job is to help clients understand what they need to know to become successful writers.

I spend my life encouraging writers to make their books as enjoyable to read as they are informative. Trying to meet that daunting challenge myself, I use humor to help the medicine go down.

Playwright Tom Stoppard once said, "Every exit is an entry someplace else." I hope that in whatever order you decide to read the book, the end of it will mark your entry into the beginning of a successful career.

A Concluding Paradox

If you knew how lucky you are to be a writer at this amazing moment in history, you wouldn't read this book. You would consecrate every waking moment to your work. Yet the better writer you are, the more you need this book to help ensure that your books earn the rewards you deserve.

DOONESBURY   by Garry Trudeau

Part One

Hiring the Agent You Need

Making the Connection

Using the Write Stuff to Find the Right Agent for You

A *Writer's Digest* cartoon shows a room full of bullet holes. Cowering on the floor in a corner is a hostage with his hands and feet tied and his mouth gagged. Next to him is a bearded young revolutionary standing in front of an open window, holding a rifle in one hand, and shouting into a megaphone, "$500,000 in tens and twenties, a plane ride to Cuba, and a good literary agent!"

It's been said that an agent is like a bank loan. You can only get one if you can prove you don't need it. Writers, editors, and agents themselves help perpetuate the greatest myth in publishing: It's hard to get an agent.

Nonsense! If you have a salable book, it's easy to get an agent, and it's easy to sell it. Writers do both all the time.

The more salable a book is, either because of its literary or commercial value, the easier these challenges are. What's really hard is making a book sell once it's published.

You find an agent the same way an agent finds a publisher: by having something salable to sell and being professional in your approach. Finding an agent is getting easier all the time. *Literary Agents of North America* lists more than a thousand agencies in thirty-eight states and Canada. If you have a marketable book project, the challenge isn't finding an agent; it's finding a competent, reputable agent with whom you feel comfortable working.

1.1   R U Redy 4 an Agt? Two Ways to Know

The moment you have a complete novel or a proposal for a nonfiction book that is 100 percent—as well conceived and crafted as you can make it—agents will be glad to hear from you. Writers sometimes ask us to read their first few chapters "to see if I should bother continuing." Getting feedback on your work is essential, but an agent's job is to sell books, not to read partial manuscripts and offer free advice about whether a writer is on the right track. The freelance editors listed in the trade directory *Literary Market Place* and agents who charge for critiquing manuscripts and are willing to consider partials will give you a written report on your book.

Until you've completed a novel, you can't prove that you can sustain plot, character, and setting for the length of a book, so a first novel usually has to be finished before an agent or publisher will consider it.

Publishers receive so many completed novels that they are usually not interested in unfinished fiction by unpublished writers. Although category romances can be sold with three chapters and an outline, this is rare with first novels. However, if you're planning a novel of 600 pages or more and you have 200 smashing pages and an extensive, dynamite outline of the plot and the characters, your book might be an exception.

Most nonfiction is sold with proposals that include information about the book and the author, an outline, and one or two sample chapters. You will find the parts of a nonfiction proposal described in appendix 4.

With children's books, don't query for a picture book; send the text. For fiction, send three chapters and a synopsis. For nonfiction, send a proposal.

Random House executive editor Kate Medina warns writers to beware of "premature emission." The two ways to know that it's time to approach an agent (or publisher) are when

1. Your proposal or manuscript is as impressive as it can be.

2. The list of things that you will do to give your book continuing national impact, especially if it's nonfiction, is as long and strong as it can be.

1.2 Can You Name That Tuna?
Seven Ways to Find an Agent

Historical romance writer June Lund Shiplett stuck a pin into the list of agents in *Literary Market Place* three times and hit my partner's name twice. That's how Elizabeth Pomada came to represent her.

Another new writer was looking for an agent in *Literary Market Place*. Her sister was on a diet, and she was making her a tuna fish casserole for her birthday. She looked at agents' names until she came to Frieda Fishbein. That's how Fishbein got to sell Colleen McCullough's best-seller, *The Thorn Birds*.

If you're not psychic or cooking for your sister's birthday, here are seven ways to look for the agent you need.

1.2.1 Your Professional Network

Ask everyone you know in the publishing business for suggestions. Chapter 15 discusses networks.

1.2.2 The Association of Authors' Representatives (AAR)

The Society of Authors' Representatives (SAR), founded in 1928, was made up of generally larger, older New York–based agencies. Founded in 1977, with our agency among the charter members, the Independent Literary Agents Association (ILAA) included newer, smaller agencies in and out of New York. In 1992, the SAR and the ILAA merged to form the Association of Authors' Representatives, Inc. (AAR). The AAR is the largest source of experienced, reputable agents. At this writing, the organization has more than 300 literary and play agents, and it continues to grow.

The AAR meets regularly to discuss issues and opportunities in publishing and related media. The association also lobbies publishers on issues of importance to writers. Members are obligated to follow the ethical guidelines reproduced in appendix 3. Although many competent, responsible agents are not members of the AAR, the association's ethical guidelines are helpful criteria for choosing and working with any agent.

For a membership list and a brochure about the role of agents, send a check or money order for $5 and a #10 business envelope with two first-class stamps to Association of Authors' Representatives, 10 Astor Place, Third Floor, New York, NY 10003. For a recorded message, call (212) 353-3709. The directories listed in the next section indicate when an agent is a member of the AAR.

1.2.3 Directories

As the number of agents grows, so does the number of reference books that list them. These directories have different strengths. They vary in the number of agents included, the kind and amount of information provided, and the advice offered about writing, agenting, and publishing.

- The *Insider's Guide to Book Editors, Publishers, and Literary Agents, 199X-199X* by AAR member Jeff Herman offers agents the chance to give prospective clients a sense of their personality by providing more than just the usual information about themselves. The *Insider's Guide* is a valuable compendium that includes information about writing, agenting, getting published, and writing a book proposal.

  The *Guide* doesn't pretend to be a complete listing of agents. Herman invited 250 agents he knows or who are members of the AAR to be listed. One hundred responded for the 1995-1996 edition, and although that is less than 10 percent of the agents in the country, the number of agents listed will continue to grow.

- *Literary Agents of North America: The Complete Guide to Over 1,000 U.S. and Canadian Literary Agencies*, edited and published by literary agents Arthur Orrmont and Leonie Rosentiel, contains the most complete list of agents on the market. It is also a unique source of information about the profession. Every edition contains a valuable overview of publishing. In addition to describing agents' interests and policies, it has indexes of the 1,000 agencies it lists by size, subject, policy and location. To order *LANA*, contact Author Aid/Research Associates International, 340 East 52nd Street, New York, NY 10022, (212) 758-4213 or (212) 980-9179.

- The *199X Guide to Literary Agents*, edited by Kirsten C. Holm and published by Writer's Digest Books, contains articles about agenting along with separate listings and subject indexes for 500 fee- and non-fee-charging agents. The guide also includes a list of script agents.

- *Literary Agents: A Writer's Guide* by Adam Begley is published in association with the New York–based group Poets and Writers. After a solid, systematic explanation of how agents work and how to find one, this guide contains a listing of almost 200 agents who do not charge to read manuscripts.

- *Literary Market Place, 199X: The Directory of the American Book Publishing Industry with Industry Yellow Pages* is the annual all-inclusive trade directory of publishing. It is put out by R. R. Bowker, the same company that publishes *Publishers Weekly*. Their list includes basic information on about 500 agents.

- *The Writer's Handbook*, which first appeared in 1936, is edited and published annually by Sylvia Burack, editor of *The Writer*. The handbook lists just the names and addresses of more than 150 agents, but it also contains articles about all kinds of writing and includes markets.

Finally, you will find the least informative but most accessible listing of agents in your area in the yellow pages.

1.2.4 Literary Events

Writing classes, seminars, and conferences; publishing courses; and book festivals present opportunities to meet or learn about agents from editors and authors. Ask if authors will let you mention their names when you contact their agents. Readings, lectures, and book signings may also yield recommendations.

1.2.5 Magazines

The Writer, Writer's Digest, Coda, and other writing magazines sometimes have articles by and about agents. So does the trade magazine *Publishers Weekly,* which also has a "Hot Deals" column and Paul Nathan's "rights" column, which describes agents' sales, a clue to how effective they are.

1.2.6 Publishers' Catalogs

Some of the seasonal catalogs that publishers use to sell their forthcoming books contain the names of the agents who control the rights on their clients' books. These catalogs are in libraries, and you can request them from publishers.

1.2.7 Books

Check the acknowledgments page of your favorite books and books related to the one you're writing. Writers sometimes thank their agents in print.

1.3 Packagers: How an Agent May Find You

The craft of packaging a book—that is, providing a publisher with a complete copyedited manuscript, a camera-ready version of the book on disk, or finished books—has created a new breed of publishing entrepreneur: the packager or book producer. Usually former editors, packagers generate fiction and nonfiction ideas for a book or a series of books, sell them with proposals, and use a network of freelancers to help them finish the project.

Editors find packagers especially helpful for series and for illustrated books that require a lot of production work. Packagers can finish a book faster and cheaper than a publisher, and they save the house's design and production staff from having to work on the project.

As you become known as a mystery writer or an authority on baseball, packagers may approach you about writing their books. The trade-off: Because they will provide the ideas, agent the books, and provide editorial help, you will earn less than you would by having your literary agent sell your work. Although you may receive royalties, you may also be writing for a fee on a work-for-hire basis.

1.4 "Dear Agent" and Other Letter Bombs

Once you have researched one or more agents whom you want to approach and you know that they handle what you write and want new clients, it's time to make contact. Regardless of how they operate, most agents prefer to be queried by mail. In the cellular age, it's been suggested that for peace of mind, what you really need is a phoneless cord. We know an exasperated agent who once bellowed, "I want to be the only agent in the country with an unlisted phone number!" If the agency is small, try calling. If you're calling long distance, mention that the agent may return the call collect. Keep time zones in mind if you call.

1.4.1 Just the Facts

Agents are endlessly besieged with letters and phone calls, so whether you call or write to an agent, be brief. For a nonfiction book, prepare a one-page query letter with three paragraphs: one about why the subject is worth a book, one about the book and what you have ready to send, and one about yourself and what you will do to promote the book.

Include anything that will convince the agent that your book will succeed, such as

- Your writing achievements

- Your media experience and contacts

- Recent coverage that will prove the media's interest in the subject (just mentioning the stories is usually enough)

- The name of a best-selling author or another well-known person who has agreed to write an introduction

- The names of nationally known opinion makers who will provide cover quotes

- Sample illustrations if they are essential

- A photograph of yourself if your appearance will be a major asset in promoting the book

- Other books you plan to write that will help sell the current one

Here are two query letters that self-destructed on sight:

Not that I compare myself with Shakespeare's Hamlet, but . . .

Dear Sir:
I have completed two novels. One is fiction. One is nonfiction.

1.4.2 Novel Ideas

For fiction, prepare a one-page letter including information about yourself and the novel. Consider starting with the opening paragraph of the novel. The ammunition just listed will also impress fiction editors. Include a synopsis describing the plot and the characters. Agents vary in how long a synopsis they prefer. My partner, Elizabeth Pomada, who handles most of the fiction in our agency, wants just one page that says what happens. A synopsis is an important selling tool that, among other things, will be used to solicit interest in Hollywood, where people don't read books.

Pat Conroy once recalled that when his hefty best-seller, *The Prince of Tides,* was being sold to the movies, one of the producer's assistants told him, "I read it last night, and it brought tears to my eyes." Pleased but surprised, Conroy asked, "You read my book last night?" "No," said the assistant, "I read the two-page treatment."

1.4.3 Letter Quality

Relating a book to a similar book that is already successful will clarify what your book is and the market for it. If, for example, your novel is a Spanish *Joy Luck Club* or a *Celestine Prophecy* set in India, an agent will know immediately what to expect.

Freelancers who sell articles with query letters know the importance of making them impeccable. Your letter is a sample of your writing. Spelling or grammatical errors or awkward, flat prose will guarantee your letter an immediate nonstop flight to the circular file. Write nothing that sounds self-serving. Let the facts prove your points.

Regard your query letter as a piece of professional writing, since that's the business the agent is in and the one you are aspiring to join. As agent Marcia Amsterdam has learned; "If they can't write a letter, they couldn't write a book."

Agents are used to receiving multiple query letters, although we do begin to wonder when we get a query addressed to "Occupant." (Just kidding.) I'm used to my last name being spelled with an *o.* However, thanks to computers, we receive queries that have the wrong address or that start, "Michael Larsen/ Elizabeth Pomada" followed by a salutation that reads: "Dear Ruth." However, AAR member Sheree Bykofsky reports, "I did get a great client this way and sold the book!"

An old advertising adage says, "You never get a second chance to make a first impression." An individually typed query creates a better impression than a photocopy, especially in the computer age. Many agents will not read past "Dear Agent" "Dear Sir/Madam," let alone "To Whom It May Concern." Returning a partial manuscript with a letter addressed to "Gentlemen," Elizabeth once wrote, "I am no gentleman!"

If it's a multiple query, mention it. In responding to a query, an agent might even suggest a more salable slant for the book. If you plan to submit your manuscript to more than one agent at a time, ask first if that's all right. Many agents won't take the time to read a complete manuscript if another agent may end up handling it.

The more income agents are earning with their present roster of clients, the less eager they are to take on new writers and the harder it will be for you to break in. However, most agents will read unsolicited queries, as distinguished from unsolicited manuscripts. A growing trend: 45 percent of the agents in *LANA* will read unsolicited faxed queries. (Include us out!) At large agencies, a query will be more likely to be read if it's addressed to a specific individual. Don't expect an answer from an agent unless you include a self-addressed postcard or a stamped #10 envelope (SASE).

Whether you call or write, don't ask to meet the agent, which some writers are anxious to do before their work has been read. Because the prevailing rejection rate is more than 90 percent, the chance that the agent will like the work is less than one out of ten, so a meeting will waste both the agent's time and yours. Agents don't want to meet with writers until they've read something they want to handle.

1.5 *Unleashing the Doggerel: How Not to Get an Agent*

R. K. Munkittrick wrote on a rejection slip to a poet who had submitted several poems to *Judge*: "Please curb your doggerel."
—Robert Henrickson, *The Literary Life and Other Curiosities*

If your book is not well enough conceived and written, you won't get an agent for it, no matter how hard you try. Let's assume that your book is well conceived and well written. All you have to do now is avoid the mistakes writers make in approaching agents. They range in severity from pet peeves to grounds for summary dismissal:

- Don't ask what agents do. Find out before contacting them.
- Don't ask an agent, "Do you take credit cards for your services?"
- Don't visit an agent without an appointment.
- Don't expect your work to be read while you wait.
- Don't start a query letter with anything but the agent's name.
- Don't use fancy typefaces.
- Don't offer a laundry list of different kinds of work.
- Don't send manuscripts or illustrations on odd-sized or colored paper.

- Don't submit a whole manuscript without asking permission.

- Don't send material that the agent doesn't handle.

- Don't say to an agent, "I have a one-thousand-page manuscript. Could you type it up for me?"

- Don't turn a page upside down in the middle of a manuscript to make sure that the agent has read it.

- Don't forget to include your address and phone number on the covering letter and the title page.

- Don't call or write before you have a book ready to sell.

- Don't call to see if a manuscript has arrived. Enclose a postcard or arrange for a return receipt.

- Don't send a messy manuscript filled with typos or errors in spelling, punctuation, or grammar, preceded by a covering letter with a plea to "please excuse the lousy typing."

- Don't call an agent at home, at night, or on weekends or holidays without permission.

- Don't call an agent while you're under the influence.

- Don't be dishonest about your work or yourself.

- Don't send a submission marked "Personal" or "Confidential."

- Don't put cute stickers, sayings, or drawings on the envelope.

- Don't take rejection personally and be rude.

- Don't expect special treatment because your manuscript is a "guaranteed best-seller."

- Don't use shipping "popcorn."

- Don't call to inform an agent that the submission you discussed on the phone has been delayed. Agents don't sit around wondering about the status of submissions they haven't received from writers they don't represent.

- Don't expect to use your advance to pay next month's rent.

- Don't query an agent on the phone and say: "My idea is so good I'm not going to tell it to you."

Remember the lesson that agents relearn every day: The more professional the writer, the better the book.

1.6 Ducking the Boomerang: How to Submit Your Manuscript

A writer named Karen Elizabeth Rigley once lamented, "Sometimes, it feels like I'm submitting boomerangs instead of manuscripts." To help avoid having agents bounce your work back at you or not return it at all, submit your manuscript properly.

Make your manuscript a document that looks like it's worth the advance you want for it. How professional a submission looks is a good indication of how well it reads.

Although some agents accept material on computer disks and queries through e-mail, more than 90 percent want hard copy. The appearance of your material reflects the professionalism with which you are approaching the agent, the subject, and your career. The way you submit your work is the tangible evidence of the care that you have taken with the proposal or manuscript. The impression of you it makes will affect readers' reactions to the project.

One of our favorite William Hamilton cartoons shows an ambitious-looking young writer confiding to a lady friend over a glass of wine: "I haven't actually been published or produced yet but I have had some things professionally typed." Whether you do it yourself or have someone else do it, make sure that your manuscript is professionally typed.

The following guidelines will make your submission as easy as possible to read for people who read reams of paper a week:

- Type your manuscript immaculately on one side of 8.5-by-11-inch white twenty-pound bond paper.

- Never use slippery, erasable, see-through onionskin.

- Type everything, including quotes and anecdotes, double-spaced.

- Avoid widows, a subhead at the bottom of a page, or the last line of a chapter at the top of a page.

- Use a standard, serif, pica—ten characters to an inch—typeface like Courier or Times Roman, a new ribbon, and clean keys. (Serif faces have cross strokes at the tops and bottoms of the letters, which make them more readable.) Avoid dot-matrix printing.

- Don't justify the right margin.

- If you have a continuous-sheet printer, use twenty-pound paper, and separate the perforated edges and the pages before mailing the manuscript.

- Type twenty-five sixty-character lines, or about 250 words on a page. Set 1.25-inch margins on the top and sides of the page.

- At the left margin of each page, half an inch from the top, type your last name and the first key word from the title. On the same line, at the right margin, type the number of the page.

"I've got all the pages numbered," bragged one writer ready to conquer the world. "Now all I have to do is fill in the rest." After you fill in the rest, be sure that your pages are numbered consecutively from the beginning to the end of the manuscript, not by chapter or the parts of a proposal. Then, if the loose pages are dropped, it will be easy to reassemble them.

Proofread your manuscript carefully, and get eagle-eyed friends to review it. One person will not spot everything. If you're using a computer, proofread a printout to catch what you may have missed on the screen, like the extra spaces that sneak in between words. Check words like *there* and *their* that spelling checker software can't. "Two bee ore not too bee" is spelled correctly! When the *its* and *it's* are wrong, someone is usually using a spelling checker.

Here are two tips for proofreading a manuscript:

1. Try proofreading the manuscript backward so you will proof the manuscript, not read it.

2. Run a finger under the words, and read them aloud softly.

Submit manuscripts unbound, without staples, paper clips, or any form of binding. Send high-quality photocopies of your text and illustrations and duplicates of slides. Never submit original artwork. Always keep a copy of everything you submit.

If you're sending a proposal, a children's book, or a short sample of the manuscript, you may use a rubber band or paper clip. For a more professional look and greater protection in case you have to resubmit the material, insert your work in the right side of a colored, double-pocket, construction-paper portfolio. Type the title and your name on a self-adhesive label, and stick it on the cover. Use the left pocket for writing samples or illustrations and an SASE. Include your name, address, and day and evening telephone numbers on the title page and on all correspondence.

If you have a computer, mention the model, the disks, and the word-processing program you use. Your publisher will probably use your disks for typesetting. However, don't send an agent disks unless he or she requests them.

Agents and publishers do not assume responsibility for lost or damaged manuscripts, so package your material neatly and carefully. For a short work, use a manila envelope or, for greater protection, a #5 mailing bag. Enclose another self-addressed, stamped mailer if you want the material returned. Never send loose stamps; they can get separated from the manuscript. Through Federal Express or United Parcel Service (UPS), you can arrange for a return envelope and postage. Without an SASE, agents or editors will probably not respond to or return your submission unless they're interested in your work.

Self-sealing envelopes and mailing bags make an agent's job easier and faster. It shouldn't take an agent longer to open the package than it does to read the manuscript. Unbelievable but true: We once received a manuscript that was wrapped in plastic, put in a box, wrapped in foil, covered in a sheet of plastic bubbles, put in another box with shredded paper, then wrapped again in brown paper and again with wire, and then the edges were taped! A manuscript packaged like this is a surefire candidate for instant incineration.

Include your covering letter and SASE inside the package with the manuscript so the agent won't have to match up your correspondence. For the same reason, don't send revisions, additions, things you left out, or address changes after you submit your book. You can't assume that agents keep a log of the thousands of submissions they reject each year. Asking agents to play matchup will not endear you to them.

Agents and editors are recycling paper, and because mailing in both directions costs more and can damage a manuscript, it may make more sense to recopy short work than ask for its return. If you don't need the material back, say so, but include a self-addressed, stamped #10 envelope if you want a response.

If you're sending a complete manuscript, pack it in a box, and use a #6 or #7 mailing bag, depending on the length of the manuscript. Five staples will seal a mailing bag effectively; avoid string or tape, and don't tape letters to the outside of the package. As AAR member Patti Breitman says, "The easier your package is to open, the easier it is for an agent to like you."

Naturally, you want to be sure that your proposal arrives, but don't call. Agents may not keep a log of incoming manuscripts, and they dislike wasting their time sifting through piles of submissions to respond to "did you get it" calls. Instead, use Federal Express or the post office's overnight service, spring for a return receipt from UPS or the post office; or use a paper clip to attach a postcard to your covering letter. Fill in your address and write this message on the back:

We received [title] on _____ .
We will get back to you by _____ .
Name: _____ .

Allow two weeks for a response to a query letter. If an agent requests a proposal or a partial or complete manuscript, find out how long the reading will take. Call or write if you haven't heard within a week or two of that time. Allow for mailing time. Don't try to guess when you sent your material. Either keep a copy of the letter handy, or note on your calendar the date it was mailed and the follow-up date as a reminder.

A six- to eight-week turnaround is typical for an established agent, but agents vary in how quickly they process submissions. If you haven't heard in eight to ten weeks and are not satisfied with the reason why—a vacation or business trip slows an agent down—ask for the manuscript back, and notify the agent that you're submitting it elsewhere.

Calls will annoy agents, and it won't get you a faster reading. A saying on a T-shirt sums up the perpetual state of agents and editors: "God put me on Earth to accomplish a certain number of things. Right now I'm so far behind I will never die." Agents receive a steady stream of queries, proposals, and manuscripts. Priority is given to those from clients. Then they plow through the rest in the order received, unless a covering letter excites them.

With rare exceptions, the industry obeys Murphy's First Law of Publishing: "Everything takes longer than anybody wants." (Murphy's Second Law of Publishing is, of course, "Anything done to speed up the process makes it worse.") The next chapter describes what happens when the response finally arrives.

Joining the Two-Percent Club

A Crash Course on Rising from Rejection to Acceptance

One day I received a package, similar to those I use to mail manuscripts, containing my book. Instead of fighting with the tape and staples, I decided to cut it open. My seventeen-year-old son watched as shredded grey stuffing fell from the cut packaging to the floor.

"Now that's what I call a rejection," he said. "They burn the manuscript and send you the ashes."

−Marion Eckholm, Writer's Digest

2.1   A Celebration of Rejection

Over the years, I've developed a macabre fascination with rejection. The next time you're feeling bad about your work being rejected, remember the trials of these best-sellers:

- *The Good Earth* by Pearl S. Buck was returned fourteen times, but it went on to win a Pulitzer Prize.

- Norman Mailer's *The Naked and the Dead* was rejected twelve times.

- Patrick Dennis said of his autobiographical novel *Auntie Mame*, "It circulated for five years through the halls of fifteen publishers and finally ended up with Vanguard Press, which, as you can see, is rather deep into the alphabet." This illustrates why using the alphabet may be a logical but ineffective way to find the best agent or editor.

- Twenty publishers felt that Richard Bach's *Jonathan Livingston Seagull* was for the birds.

- The first title of *Catch-22* was *Catch-18*, but Simon and Schuster planned to publish it during the same season that Doubleday was bringing out *Mila 18* by Leon Uris. When Doubleday complained, Joseph Heller changed the title. Why 22? Because Simon and Schuster was the 22nd publisher to read it. *Catch-22* has become part of the language and has sold more than 10 million copies.

- Mary Higgins Clark was rejected forty times before selling her first story. One editor wrote: "Your story is light, slight and trite." More than 30 million copies of her books are now in print.

- Before he wrote *Roots*, Alex Haley had received 200 rejections.

- Robert Pirsig's classic, *Zen and the Art of Motorcycle Maintenance*, couldn't get started at 121 houses.

- John Grisham's first novel, *A Time to Kill*, was declined by fifteen publishers and some thirty agents. His novels have more than 60 million copies in print.

- Thirty-three publishers couldn't digest *Chicken Soup for the Soul*, compiled by Jack Canfield and Mark Victor Hansen, before it became a huge best-seller and spawned a series.

- The *Baltimore Sun* hailed *Naked in Deccan* as "a classic" after it had been rejected over seven years by 375 publishers.

- Zelda wouldn't marry F. Scott Fitzgerald until he sold a story. He papered his bedroom walls with rejection slips before he won her hand.

- Dr. Seuss's first book was rejected twenty-four times. The sales of his children's books have soared to 100 million copies.

- Louis L'Amour received 200 rejections before he sold his first novel. During the last forty years, Bantam has shipped nearly 200 million of his 112 books, making him their biggest selling author.

- If you visit the House of Happy Walls, Jack London's beautiful estate in Sonoma County, north of San Francisco, you will see some of the 600 rejection slips that London received before selling his first story. If you want to know how much easier it is to make it as a writer now than it was in London's time, read his wonderful autobiographical novel, *Martin Eden*. Your sufferings will pale compared to what poor Martin endured.

- British writer John Creasy received 774 rejections before selling his first story. He went on to write 564 books, using fourteen names.

- Eight years after his novel *Steps* won the National Book Award, Jerzy Kosinski permitted a writer to change his name and the title and send a manuscript of the novel to thirteen agents and fourteen publishers to test the plight of new writers. They all rejected it, including Random House, which had published it.

Throughout this book, you will see humorous rejections from my collection. If you're going to be in any of the creative arts, you have to take heart from poet Robert Service's belief that "rebuffs are merely rungs on the ladder of success." Look at rejection as *selection*, as a way of helping you pick the right agent and editor for you. Console yourself with best-selling author Joe Girard's maxim: "Every no gets you closer to yes."

2.2   The Right to Be Wrong: Why Manuscripts Are Rejecteb

Rejection is 100 percent guaranteed in the writing profession.
     –Gregg Levoy, This Business of Writing

Agents reject submissions for many reasons that have nothing to do with the quality of the work. Here is an incomplete list of the reasons agents may reject your work:

- There are too many typos or grammatical errors.
- The writing isn't strong enough.
- The subject or kind of novel is too hard to sell.
- The book is not for the general public.
- Not enough houses publish that kind of book.
- The submission doesn't look professional.
- The timing is wrong for the market.
- The subject has too much competition.
- Your work competes with that of one of the agent's clients.

- The agent doesn't handle the kind of work you have submitted.

- The agent is in a bad mood, ill, too busy, or too successful to be receptive to your work.

- The book is too depressing.

- It won't help readers enough.

- The work doesn't have enough subsidiary-rights potential. (Chapter 8 discusses subsidiary rights.)

Only the first two of these reasons relates to the quality of your proposal or manuscript. All of the others have nothing to do with how good your book is. Remember: An agent isn't rejecting *you*, just your work.

If an agent rejects your query or manuscript, go on to the next agent. Assume that the first agent is shortsighted, but don't expect an explanation about why your submission was rejected.

"I know it's not perfect," you may be tempted to reply, "but how am I going to make it better if agents won't tell me what's wrong with it?"

To which an agent (or editor) might respond, "Telling you what's wrong with it is not my job until we're working together. If you're not paying for my time, how can I justify adding to the time I've wasted reading your work by telling you why and risk giving you the impression that I want to start a dialogue? What I want is to find the next salable manuscript as quickly as possible."

(If you didn't notice the typo in the heading of this section, write the word *rejected* five times on the blackboard.)

2.3 Going in Style: A California Rejection

A writer at the Santa Barbara Writer's Conference once quipped that people become agents for the same reason that they become dentists: They like to inflict pain. Yet when it comes to enduring rejection, nobody can top literary agents.

Being writers as well as agents, Elizabeth and I are especially sensitive to rejection. Here is the rejection letter that we send out:

Dear Writer:

Alas, we must reject what you have been kind enough to submit to us. We only handle adult book-length fiction and nonfiction, and either you submitted something else, or in today's difficult publishing market, we are unable to see how we can help you achieve the success that you want for your book.

Like the rest of the arts, publishing is a very subjective business. Even though we have written or coauthored thirteen books, most of which have been successful, we still get rejected.

Although we have sold books to more than ninety publishers since 1972, our clients' work is still rejected. Nor do all of the books that we do sell succeed.

Like editors, we love to get excited about new books and promising writers. Nonetheless, the hardest part of our job is finding books to sell, and it's getting harder.

We would like to respond to each submission we receive with a personal letter. But like editors, we receive thousands of them a year and reject more than 90 percent of them, which forces us to use this form letter.

Rejecting manuscripts that later become best-sellers is a publishing tradition. So we hope that you will assume that we are wrong and that you will persevere until your books reach the goals that you have set for them.

We usually can't suggest another agent or a publisher who might be interested in a writer's work, but directories of publishers and agents and your professional network will lead you in the right direction. Persistence rewards talent.

Thank you for giving our agency the opportunity to represent you. We wish you the best of luck with your writing career.

Yours for Good Books That Sell (Especially When They're Yours!),

Michael Larsen   Elizabeth Pomada

2.4   Sailboats and Recipes: How to Make Your Submission Stand Out

As Jeff Herman notes in the *Insider's Guide to Book Editors, Publishers, and Literary Agents*, "Most agents are rejecting 98 percent of the opportunities that cross their desks." Writers ask us how they can join the 2-percent club, how they can make their submissions stand out and rise to the top of the pile faster. Consider these suggestions, which supplement the recommendations in chapter 1 for what to include in a query letter:

- Start your query letter with the name of one of the agent's clients—the more valuable, the better.

- Offer a fresh, unique, original, highly commercial idea.

- Make your writing irresistible.

- Include the number of cities that you will visit to promote your book.

- Mention the number of books that you will personally sell a year.

- Indicate how much you will spend for promotion.

- Include the number of copies of the book that companies have agreed to buy.

- Make the agent laugh.

- Come up with a brilliant title.

- Imbue your writing with your voice so that your personality shines through.

- Indicate that it's a single submission, and explain why you are eager to work with the agent.

- Include an effective cover design to help interest the agent.

- Be passionate about other books, especially any that the agent represents that are like yours.

- Include an attention-getting device. Someone once sent us a flower pot with five-foot-high dried branches sticking out of it and fake $100 bills hanging from the branches to suggest that his book was going to be an evergreen money tree. Imagination is far more important than cost. Aim for something small and relevant that you can include with your submission. When Bay Area agent Jillian Manus submitted a proposal on assertiveness for women, she included a whip and a note saying, "Submit to your editor."

- Don't try to bribe an agent. A gift before a sale will feel like a bribe, and it will be counterproductive with a responsible agent. However, agents can be seduced by the prospect of something nice, relevant, and out-of-the-ordinary. If your book relates to sailing or the sea and you own a boat, suggest discussing your book under full sail. If you're writing about food, don't send homemade food, but if you own a restaurant, inviting the agent to sample your favorite recipe would be an enjoyable way to begin your relationship. Again, the goal is relevance and imagination, not making a financial sacrifice to impress an agent. (Note: The cost of these gambits is tax-deductible.)

The thread that runs through these suggestions is imagination: doing something creative. However, these ideas will only help you if you can convince an agent that you have a salable book. None of them is necessary. If you do none of them but have a salable book, you'll still find an agent.

There's another way to receive a faster reading. If the agent is in a city that you will be traveling to, the agent may be willing to consider the manuscript before you arrive so that you can meet if the agent is interested.

2.5   A Hitchhiker's Guide to Asking the Right Questions

One summer while I was going to college, I hitchhiked from New York to San Francisco. It enabled me to experience for the first time how vast, gorgeous, and for the most part empty the United States is. Being an agent is like looking for a job or being a hitchhiker. If you're out there on the road with your thumb out and you look harmless, strangers will take a chance on you. Many cars will pass you by before one stops, and you never know how long or enjoyable the ride will be, but sooner or later you'll find the rides you need to reach your destination.

A writer in search of an agent is also like a hitchhiker on the publishing highway holding up a manuscript in the hope of being picked up by an agent and a publisher. A new writer is especially susceptible to being taken for a ride by a bad agent—a fate worse than having no agent.

Research the agents that you are approaching through your professional network and the directories listed in the first chapter. Ask if they have guidelines, a brochure, or a list of recent sales that they can send you. If they do, send them a #10 SASE for it. Agent Arthur Pine sends out a complete list of his published titles.

When an agent likes your work and wants to represent you, meet him or her if you can. It will be easier for you to size up an agent and establish a rapport in person than over the phone.

Meeting an agent is a chemistry test that both of you have to pass. Visiting will also give you a tax-deductible chance to see the office and the books that the agent has sold, and to meet the staff.

There's no certainty that your courtship will lead to a happy working marriage, but prospects for a successful relationship will be enhanced if you are familiar with your agent's experience, personality, and operating procedures. You should know what the agent will do for you and what you need from the agent.

The AAR offers the following helpful guide on what to ask an agent who wants to represent you. (Do not, as one writer did, send this list with your query letter!)

Suggested Agent Checklist for Authors

The following is a suggested list of topics for authors to discuss with literary agents with whom they are entering into a professional relationship.

1. Is your agency a sole proprietorship? A partnership? A corporation?

2. Are you a member of the Association of Authors' Representatives?

3. How long have you been in business as an agent?

4. How many people does your agency employ?

5. Of the total number of employees, how many are agents, as opposed to clerical workers?

6. Do you have specialists at your agency who handle movie and television rights? Foreign rights? Do you have sub-agents or corresponding agents overseas and in Hollywood?

7. Do you represent other authors in my area of interest?

8. Who in your agency will actually be handling my work? Will other staff members be familiar with my work and the status of my business at your agency? Will you oversee or at least keep me apprised of the work that your agency is doing on my behalf?

9. Do you issue an agent-author contract? May I review a specimen copy? And may I review the language of the agency clause that appears in contracts you negotiate for your clients?

10. What is your approach to providing editorial input and career guidance for your clients or for me specifically?

11. How do you keep your clients informed of the activities on their behalf? Do you regularly send them copies of publishers' rejection letters? Do you provide them with submission lists and rejection

letters on request? Do you regularly, or upon request, send out updated activity reports?

12. Do you consult with your clients on any and all offers?

13. Some agencies sign subsidiary contracts on behalf of their clients to
expedite processing. Do you?

14. What are your commissions for: (1) basic sales to U.S. publishers,
(2) sales of movie and television rights, (3) audio and multimedia
rights, (4) British and foreign translation rights?

15. What are your procedures and time frames for processing and dis-
bursing client funds? Do you keep different bank accounts separat-
ing author funds from agency revenue?

16. What are your policies about charging clients for expenses incurred
by your agency? Will you list such expenses for me? Do you advance
money for such expenses?

17. How do you handle legal, accounting, public relations, or similar
services that fall outside the normal range of a literary agent's functions?

18. Do you issue 1099 tax forms at the end of each year? Do you also
furnish clients upon request with a detailed account of their financial activity, such as gross income, commissions and other deduc-
tions, and net income for the past year?

19. In the event of your death or disability, or the death or disability of
the principal person running the agency, what provisions exist for
continuing operation of my account, for the processing of money
due to me, and for the handling of my book and editorial needs?

20. If we should part company, what is your policy about handling any
unsold subsidiary rights to my work that were reserved to me under
the original publishing contracts?

21. What are your expectations of me as a client?

22. Do you have a list of do's and don'ts for your clients that will enable
me to help you do your job better?

The following questions will also help you find out about the agent's
personality and credentials:

- How did you become an agent?
- What kinds of books do you handle?
- Who are some of the publishers to whom you have sold books?
- About how many clients do you handle?

Personal relationships with editors are essential, so if the agent is outside of New York, ask how often he or she visits editors in New York.

Top cookbook agent Martha Jane Casselman, an AAR member, suggests that one way to check an agent's credentials in your field is to ask if he or she is a member of the relevant professional groups.

Taken together, the answers to these questions should help you determine whether you are talking to an experienced agent.

The following questions will help define your working relationship:

- Will you receive a commission on short pieces that I sell?
- What are the chances of your selling my book?
- How long do you think it will take?
- How much of an advance should I expect for my book?
- How will you go about placing the book?
- When would you like me to contact you?
- When should I expect to hear from you?

You don't have to ask these particular questions or limit yourself to them. Directories will provide some of the answers. When an agent expresses an interest in taking you on, satisfy yourself before you agree—as you would before hiring a doctor, lawyer, or accountant—that the agent can and wants to represent you.

The bigger the agents are and the more modest the books they are asked to represent, the less amenable they will be about having to prove themselves to new writers. No agent likes to be grilled, but you don't want an agent who's half-baked. When it comes to getting to know your agent, style is as important as content. During your first conversation, ask only about what you need to know but can't learn from other sources.

If an agent promises you the moon, head for the nearest exit. If the agent decides not to represent you, tactfully ask why. You may not change the agent's mind, but the feedback may help with your next interview.

2.6   If Once Is Not Enough: Interviewing More Than One Agent

A store in San Francisco once sold T-shirts that read, "Life is one audition after another." Should you interview more than one agent before making a choice? No and maybe.

You can send multiple query letters and multiple samples of a novel, informing the agents that it's a multiple submission. However, most agents will take the time to read a whole manuscript only if they have it on an exclusive basis. So if more than one agent requests the whole manuscript, research the agents enough to pick the one that you that would most like to represent you. If the relationship doesn't work out, go on to the next agent who asked to see the manuscript.

If you're writing nonfiction, you can send multiple queries, and you can send proposals to more than one agent at a time if they consent. If more than one agent wants to represent you, researching the agents in directories and through your professional network may help you decide which agent to choose.

If you're still not sure, try to gauge the agent's interest and passion by talking to them on the phone. Ask to see copies of their agency agreements. If you're still not sure and an agent accepts your interviewing others at the same time, go to it.

Interviews will help you decide, but they will also waste all but one agent's time. If you are approaching new agents whose ability you are unsure of, it would be justified, but experienced agents have already proven themselves. They may feel that if they're willing to risk their time and overhead on a new writer, they shouldn't have to audition for the opportunity.

Talking to an agent's clients may not be helpful. For one thing, agents may not want their writers bothered by prospective clients looking for recommendations. In addition, present clients are going to be happy with their agents, which is why they're still clients. Writers who have left their agents may be unfairly biased against them and unable to provide you with an objective assessment. As with any kind of marriage, you may encounter writers who have had wonderful or horrendous experiences with the same person.

Be as professional in approaching an agent as you are in your writing and as you expect your agent to be with you. Whatever an agent says or does should make as much sense to you as it does to the agent. Trust your instincts and your common sense.

A Study in Read and Green

Six Criteria for Choosing the Right Agent for You

Dream Job Opportunity
Literary Agents Needed Now

Start a new high-income, low-risk career today. Enter the glamorous, high-stakes world of big-time publishing. No experience, training, testing, or degree necessary. Salary potential unlimited. If you have a telephone, you can be a literary agent now!

Be in constant demand by America's millions of writers. Get paid to read future best-sellers. Meet new people anxious to know you. Be wined and dined at glamorous restaurants by New York editors eager to work with you. Get invited to chic publishing parties. Feast on juicy gossip.

Become indispensable to eternally grateful authors. Have books dedicated to you. Make a fortune with your stable of best-selling authors. Become a power broker in the industry. Be quoted in columns. Have stories written about you. Sell your books to the movies and meet the stars. Write your memoirs.

Set your own hours. Sleep late. Wear whatever you like. Take long vacations. Don't delay. Start the moment your business cards arrive.

Realists need not apply.

3.1 How Agents Become Agents

The 2,500 literary agents in the country's 1,000 agencies succumbed to the lure of this imaginary ad, even though they never saw it. If you like books, have an entrepreneurial spirit, and perhaps a working spouse, being a literary agent is tempting. Discovering wonderful new writers and helping them get their books published is a noble ambition.

Of course, there are some days when, if agents were asked how they became agents, they would answer: "Just unlucky, I guess." However, most agents, like most editors, do the job for love, not money. They do it because they like books and they like people. Johnny Carson once defined an optimist as an accordionist with a beeper. Agents are eternal optimists.

Literary agents are as diverse, independent, and individualistic as the writers they represent. Just as anyone is free to write books, anyone may agent them. All you need to call yourself an agent is a desk, stationery, office supplies, a computer, a telephone, a fax machine, and an address (a post office box will do). This explains why many agents (including us), who may think big but start small, work out of their homes.

AAR member Sandra Dijkstra, who represents Susan Faludi and Amy Tan, believes that becoming an agent is only a matter of Cartesian logic. French philosopher René Descartes believed, "I think, therefore I am." Aspiring entrepreneurs around the country are saying to themselves, "I think I'm an agent, therefore I *am* an agent." Only time and their bank accounts will tell if they are right.

The low start-up costs, lack of licensing requirements (except for movie agents), deceptive simplicity of the business, and glamorous aura of publishing attract would-be agents. Consequently, agents vary enormously in their qualifications and operating procedures.

There are many ways to become an agent. The traditional path to agenting—and still the best one—goes around an editor's desk. As you will see in chapter 13, your editor is the in-house agent for your book. An agent who has been an editor of adult fiction and nonfiction at a large trade publisher has a big head start in gaining the experience needed for the job.

Working for major publishers in other positions will also provide on-the-job training in how publishing works and the opportunity to learn skills that agents need. Successful agents have learned about the business as sales representatives, subsidiary-rights salespeople, publicists, promotion directors, house counsels, and in other positions.

After being an editor, the second best way to learn how to be an agent is to work for one. At the bicoastal William Morris agency, aspiring agents start out in the mail room. Sheree Bykofsky became an agent while working for a packager. After selling four books in one month, she incorporated.

Working in a bookstore enables book lovers to learn on the front lines what sells and what dies. This is excellent experience for developing a sense of the kinds of books that sales reps can convince booksellers to stock and what motivates people to spend their hard-earned money on books.

Lawyers who become agents may not have a publishing background, but they bring a knowledge of contracts and negotiation that makes them effective at the bargaining table.

These are only the most obvious ways to learn about agenting, but there are many others such as being an author or a writing teacher or working in the movie business or in other media as a magazine editor or a journalist.

Would-be agents who join the ranks without either publishing experience or ability account for much of the turnover in the agency business. Like writers, the survivors all toil at the same job, but no two of them do it exactly alike.

Steve Allen once returned a manuscript sent by a hopeful writer, with the following note, "I thought you'd like to see what some fool is sending out under your name."

3.2 How the Author Became an Agent and Then Became the Author

My partner, Elizabeth Pomada, and I did promotion work for six major New York houses before moving to San Francisco in 1970, giving us a ready-made network when we set up our agency two years later. Patty Hearst made me an agent. I had been consulting with Elizabeth on books she was handling, but when the story of Hearst's abduction broke in February 1974, I knew that there was a book in it. So I called Tim Findley, one of the two reporters who were collaborating on the page-one stories in the *San Francisco Chronicle*, and asked if he wanted to write a book. He said no, so I called the other reporter, Paul Avery, who said maybe.

I called Bantam, where I had worked, to see if they wanted to do an instant book on the Symbionese Liberation Army (SLA). They declined. So I called Bill Grose at Dell, who said yes. I had just sold a book with four phone calls, an exhilarating experience.

The deal was consummated at about the time of the fiery Los Angeles shoot-out that May, so we envisioned an instant book that would immortalize the meteoric rise and fall of the SLA. Unfortunately, Hearst wasn't captured for nineteen months.

When she was finally apprehended, we held Avery and his collaborator, Vin McLellan, hostage in our apartment for two weeks as they worked day and night finishing the manuscript. We had an extra bed in our hallway and alternating typists going around the clock.

By that time, though, half a dozen books had come and gone, and Dell was no longer interested in a quickie. So we resold it to Putnam as a hardcover. *The Voices of Guns* came out in early 1977, three years after the event that produced it. Although *Voices* was first-rate, it sank like a stone. It arrived too late. The public had already learned more about the story from the media than it wanted to know. A television movie company paid for three option periods, but that, too, came to naught.

Besides being an exciting introduction to agenting and a book of which we remain very proud, *Voices* was a lesson about the hazards of doing topical books. The situation also presents an unusual example of how far agents are willing to go to help finish a book.

You are reading these words because Carol Cartaino, then editor in chief at Writer's Digest Books, read *Painted Ladies*, our first book about Victorian houses, and took a chance on asking a San Francisco agent to write about a profession based in New York. PJ Dempsey, a senior editor at John Wiley & Sons who started a line of books about writing, brought *Literary Agents* back to life after Writer's Digest Books let it go out of print. How's that for a chain of accidents?

The single most abominable rejection I have ever heard of a writer receiving was this: "Dear Mr. Andrews: We cannot use the paper you sent us. You wrote on it."

—Gregg Levoy, *This Business of Writing*

3.3 Mix and Stir: The Ingredients for a Working Marriage

What are the qualifications for being an agent? The relationship between a writer and an agent, like that between a writer and an editor, is a working marriage. The personal qualities needed include the same virtues that help sustain any marriage: honesty, intelligence, compassion, friendliness, trust, patience, confidence, initiative, responsiveness, reliability, perserverance, promptness, courtesy, respect, enthusiasm, chemistry, a sense of humor, loyalty, faith in you and your work, the ability to stand up for yourself, and optimism tinged with fatalism.

As a professional, an agent needs to have

- A knowledge and love of writing and books and the desire and ability to represent different kinds of books and authors to different kinds of editors and publishers
- The ability to keep track of a changing mélange of books, meetings, phone calls, clients, correspondence, submissions from writers and to editors, deals, projects in different forms and stages, editors and other in-house people, subsidiary-rights contacts, and contacts in the trade and consumer media
- The ability to judge books and advise writers how to make their work more salable
- A knowledge of and interest in the publishing business
- A knowledge of and credibility with editors and subsidiary-rights buyers
- A knowledge of contracts and how to negotiate them
- The ability and willingness to be tough on a writer's behalf
- Curiosity about anything that could wind up between covers
- Persistence and creativity in trying to sell a property and in following up afterward on royalty statements and subsidiary-rights sales
- The recognition that helping to shape a writer's career is a serious responsibility that one must continue to live up to if one expects to keep a client

3.4   Their Way or the Highway: Why Agents Are Like Books

Every book is a book, yet every book is different. So it is with agents. They vary in their personalities, their backgrounds, and the size and location of their agencies. This leads to a wide spectrum of approaches to running a business. Agents vary in

- Their competence
- The books they handle
- The number of writers they handle
- Whether they accept queries by phone, fax, mail or e-mail

- What they request in an initial submission

- How involved they get with the publishing process which may vary from book to book and author to author

- How they submit books

- The number of editors and publishers with whom they deal

- How many publishers they try before giving up on a project

- Whether they charge fees, what they charge them for, how much they are, and what the fees buy

- Their commissions

- Whether their agency agreement is oral or written

- The terms of their agreements (which are discussed in chapter 4)

- When they're available to clients

- The amount of contact they like to have with clients

Agents also vary in how long they take to respond to submissions, from ten days or even less to two months or longer for established agents. Their response time depends on whether they are responding to a letter, sample material, a nonfiction proposal, or a complete manuscript and, of course, on how excited they are about the submission or the author.

A woman submitted a novel to an agent, and two months later, she called to see what had happened to it. The agent drew a blank.

"Was it a romance?" he asked.

"No," she said.

"Was it a mystery?"

"No."

"Was it historical?"

"Well," said the writer, "it wasn't when I sent it."

Agents' tastes, interests, and literary judgments also vary. They vary in how strongly they have to feel about a project to handle it. Some agents will only represent work they love. Others live by the Hollywood adage, "Sell it, don't smell it."

Agents may specialize in children's books, nonfiction, or literary, commercial, or genre fiction, such as romances or science fiction. However, most can't afford to or don't want to specialize and will consider adult fiction and nonfiction for the general public. Many agents will consider young adult and children's books. Some handle textbooks, articles, short stories, and even poetry. *Literary Agents of North America* and the *Guide to Literary Agents and Art/Photo Reps* include subject indexes.

Looking for an agent can be, as Bay Area agent Claudia Hagadus Long lamented, "depressing and intimidating." Answering the following questions will ease the strain by enabling you to identify the kind of agent you want to represent you. When you find an agent willing to work with you, the answers will help you assess the likelihood of a happy marriage.

3.5 What Qualities Do You Need in an Agent?

Whether you are looking for your first spouse or your first agent, what you need from the relationship may be hard to judge. To help avoid being disappointed, try to figure out the kind of relationship you want with an agent, and then find one whom you think will satisfy your needs.

Martha Casselman, an AAR member, speaks for her colleagues when she says, "I'm somewhere between a lawyer and a shrink." A writer once confessed to Carolyn Marino, editor in chief of HarperPaperbacks: "John Doe's my agent, but I'm afraid to call him." If you need a lot of personal attention or hand-holding, don't choose an agent who prefers to keep the relationship strictly business.

It's been said that 70 percent of what is remembered when you talk to someone is not what you say but everything else about you: your appearance, the tone of your voice, and your friendliness. Friendliness is a quality that is essential for some agents, unimportant for others. One of the top agents in the business once told me that he had no interest in being friends with his clients. His job was to make money for them, and that was his sole concern.

If you want a shark in your corner, find one. A writer once gushed to me about her well-known agent: "I love him. He's the only person I know who's meaner than I am." In *Beyond the Bestseller*, Richard Curtis's excellent inside portrait of publishing, he refers to a successful agent "with a tongue like a trash can."

A client of another well-known agent was talking to a friend about her agent, and the friend said, "Everyone says she's a bitch." "Yes," the client replied, "but she's *my* bitch."

3.6   Do You Want a Large, Medium-Sized, or Small Agency?

Most literary agencies are one- or two-person shops. *Literary Agents of North America* lists more than 100 medium-sized agencies that have three to six people on staff. The twenty large agencies in *LANA* with eight or more people have subsidiary-rights specialists for first-serial sales, movie, foreign, and electronic rights.

Two large agencies, William Morris and International Creative Management (ICM), have offices in New York and Los Angeles and abroad. They represent actors, screenwriters, producers, and directors whom they can call on to "package" a movie deal, that is, to bring all the talent together to get financing for a movie.

Large agencies have lawyers on staff who review and negotiate contracts, which may save writers legal fees. Whereas agents in small agencies have to monitor their clients' financial affairs themselves, large agencies have accounting departments that enable the agents to concentrate on selling. These high-powered agencies have overheads to match their clout and are more eager to find commercial properties, or those that they can recycle in other media, than they are interested in small projects with little subsidiary-rights potential.

A writer once came to us after leaving the top man at a large agency. He felt that he was neglected there because he was a "small fish in a big pond." As another writer delicately put it, "I believe my potatoes were too small for their baronial tables."

My brother, Ray, has helped produce a number of Broadway plays and won a Tony for *Mornings at Seven*. One year, he gave us tickets to the Tony Awards. Before the show began, producer Alexander Cohen remarked that "pneumonia is a cold managed by the William Morris Agency." The prestige of being represented by a large agency like ICM, William Morris, Curtis Brown (which also has an office in San Francisco), Janklow & Nesbit, or Sterling Lord Literistic helps open doors for clients. Editors may offer agents at large agencies larger advances than they would offer small agencies for the same book. In *Writing the Blockbuster Novel*, AAR member Al Zuckerman of Writers House estimates that about twenty agents account for 90 percent of the best-selling novels.

At the same time, publishers are buying books, not agents, and they will pay any agent whatever it takes to acquire a book they want. What agents bring to the table is the ability to judge what a book is worth and to extract that sum from an eager publisher. Zuckerman believes that agents, caught between authors wanting to be paid more for their books and editors wanting to pay less, have to have the best judgment about what a book is really worth.

The risk of poor communication arises between the writer and the agent in large agencies because different agents who may be on opposite coasts handle various rights. You can minimize this problem by establishing effective lines of communication with your primary agent, the one who takes you on.

Your goal is to find an agent you will enjoy working with and who will do an effective job for you. If your book is salable enough, you will find an eager agent at an agency of any size. Whether you choose to look for a big, medium-sized, or small agency will depend on you and your assessment of your book.

However, if you are a new writer, you may find that small agencies are:

- More open to "small" books and unpublished writers

- More accessible by phone

- Less harried, especially if they're out of the pressure-cooker atmosphere of the Big Apple

- More able to respond quickly to your submission

- More likely to be concerned about the quality of your relationship as well as the salability of your work

3.7   Are You Willing to Pay a Reading Fee?

Back in the days before paperback auctions, agents' megabuck demands, and conglomerate mergers, publishing was a nice, quiet "gentleman's business." Even today, unobtrusive gentility is still expected of agents in acquiring clients. This is true despite a new breed of agents who regard stealing clients as just another part of the job.

Literary agents expect clients to find them through directory listings, referrals, and their presence at literary events. Advertising, although legal, is frowned on; so are reading fees. The Association of Authors' Representatives responded to concerns about fees by deciding that members cannot charge them. Arthur Orrmont, coeditor of *Literary Agents of North America*, reported that when he receives complaints from writers, he drops agents from *LANA* who are unethical about charging very high editorial or retainer fees.

There are, however, able, responsible agents who charge reading fees and may even edit your manuscript for a fee or a larger commission. You cannot expect an agent who doesn't charge a fee to edit your work. You have to make sure that it's impeccable before submitting it.

Most successful agents keep track of expenses incurred on their authors' behalf and either deduct these fees as their income is received or bill their clients if there is no income from which to deduct the expenses.

Like editors, established agents receive thousands of submissions a year and reject more than 90 percent of them. Regardless of whether they earn a living from agenting, agents may feel entitled to a fee for the time spent reading and critiquing what they regard as unsalable work. Some agents just charge unpublished writers, some refund the fee if they decide to handle the book or if it is sold.

When Elizabeth and I started our agency in 1972, we wanted to see everything. After a year or so, we realized that we had read more than 150 manuscripts and found only two worth handling. To stanch the flow and, we naively hoped, improve the quality of submissions, we decided to charge a $25-dollar fee for reading complete manuscripts, which is what Elizabeth was being paid to review books for the *San Francisco Chronicle*, and to refund the fee if we handled the project. Alas, the jewels and refunded fees were few, and after a year or so, we could no longer afford the time.

We don't charge reading fees now, but we start by looking at only the first thirty pages and a synopsis of a completed novel or a proposal for nonfiction. Even that is farther than most editors go if they're wading through the slush pile of unsolicited manuscripts. One respected New York agent only asks for the first two pages and a synopsis of a novel.

If you're dead set against paying a reading fee, don't. More than half of the agents listed in the fifth edition of *LANA* don't charge one. However, charging a fee doesn't automatically brand an agent as dishonest.

To check if fee-charging agents are reputable, ask what percentage of their income they earn from reading and editing, as opposed to sales of books. The percentage will be greater for a new agent, which doesn't mean that the agent isn't reputable. However, if the agency has been in business for a decade and still derives most of its income from fees, beware.

Before sending your work to an agency that charges a reading fee, find out if additional fees are required for editing or reading a revision, whether you will receive a critique of your manuscript, and if and when the agent refunds the fee. Be a wary consumer, as you are with any new product or service you try, until you're convinced that you are dealing with an experienced, reputable agency.

More than half of the agents listed in *LANA* charge clients for costs or services. At one point, however, one agent was asking writers to pay a 15-percent commission, $100 a month, a minimum contribution of $100 for a trip to New York, and for dinners the agent had with editors. The author was also expected to do the initial mailing of the manuscript at the agent's direction.

There is nothing illegal about this because agents are free to work any way they want. It's been said that you have to risk your life to feel alive. Agenting books is rarely life threatening, but there's usually an element of risk.

Writers risk their time writing their books, agents risk theirs by trying to sell them. Traditionally, agents' basic overhead, apart from expenses arising directly from representing their authors, has come out of their income, not their writers'. If the book doesn't sell, both are out the time, effort, and overhead they gambled on the project. This remains the premise of the writing and agenting professions.

Risk is one of the most exciting aspects of writing, agenting, and publishing. Books by best-selling authors sometimes fail, and new writers like Robert *(Bridges)* Waller and John *(Men Are from Mars)* Gray come out of nowhere and build a nest on the best-seller list. Maybe your book will be one of the surprises.

3.8   *What Commission Are You Willing to Pay?*

A cartoon once showed a group of agents sitting around a table. One of them says, "We've got to figure out a way to keep these damn writers from getting 90 percent of our income!"

More than half of the agents listed in *LANA* have found a way to increase their income. They have raised their commission from 10 to 15 percent.

The agenting profession started in England in the late nineteenth century because of

- The mistreatment of authors by publishers

- The growing value and complexity of subsidiary rights in England and America

- The protection of authors' rights provided by the first American copyright law

In the 1880s, a lawyer in London named A. P. Watt used to bill authors for his services. When they didn't pay, he had his authors' earnings sent to him, deducted a 10 percent commission, and then forwarded the balance to the authors. Paul Reynolds, the first American agent, began his fifty-two-year career in 1891.

Mark Twain was one of the first American authors to have an agent. In the United States, the number of agents started to grow after World War I. With few exceptions, the 10-percent commission held firm until the 1970s.

The rise in commissions accelerated during the recession in the early eighties. Hit by rising costs, shrinking advances and royalties, lower bookstore sales, a proliferation of agents, and the greater difficulty of selling books to penny-pinching publishers, agents were pushed into raising their commissions. Just as publishers raised their prices, agents started to raise their commissions. Agents have increased their commissions out of need, not greed, and some (including us) are absorbing costs—such as postage, long-distance telephone calls, and perhaps photocopying—previously charged to authors.

Literary agents are free to charge whatever writers are willing to pay them. (Movie and talent agents are limited by law to 10 percent.) Agents who provide editorial assistance may charge a commission as high as 25 percent. Rosalie Heacock, an AAR member in Santa Monica, California, charges 15 percent of the first $50,000 a year and 10 percent thereafter. The commission you pay should seem fair to you.

3.9   How Important Is an Agent's Experience?

> Judgment is what you get from experience. Good judgment is what you get from bad experience.
>
> –Anonymous

Should you sign up with a new agent or approach those who have been around a while? An agent's stock-in-trade is his or her contacts; knowledge of writing, books, publishing, contracts, and selling subsidiary rights; and the ability to work with writers and publishers. An agent can acquire much of this knowledge only through experience. However, publishing experience doesn't guarantee you an effective agent, and the lack of it doesn't preclude someone from becoming an accomplished agent if he or she is capable of learning the trade.

There is a trade-off between established agents and new ones. Although the former bring skill and experience to the table, new agents may respond quicker, and they may have more eagerness to make a name for themselves, more passion for a project, more time to devote to editing it, and more zeal for selling it. These things can make up for the difference in experience.

Unless you have confidence in your agent's ability to negotiate a contract and unless your agent has negotiated deals of the same size as yours, ask him or her to consult with a more experienced agent or a knowledgeable literary lawyer to ensure that the contract will be as finely tuned as possible when it reaches you.

3.10 Does Your Agent Have to Be in the Big Apple?

> New York is the first, second, third and fourth worlds all rolled into one.
>
> —Gloria Steinem

New York harbors the greatest concentration of literary agents in the world. However, Patti Breitman in San Anselmo, California; Jane Jordan Browne in Chicago; Sandra Dijkstra in Del Mar, California; Frederick Hill in San Francisco and Los Angeles; Raphael Sagalyn in Washington, D.C.; and Lucinda Vardey in Toronto are proving that agents don't have to be in the Big Apple to flourish. As mentioned earlier, *LANA* lists agents in thirty-eight states.

Ultimately, agents don't sell books, and writers don't sell books. Books sell books. The power of agents and publishers comes from the words of their writers. An editor reads a proposal or a manuscript and decides from a literary or commercial point of view, ideally both, that the book is worth publishing. It makes no difference whether the manuscript arrives from across the street or across the country or even whether it comes from an agent.

One of the reasons that New York is the capital of the world is its unique concentration of radio and television networks, trade and consumer print media, book publishers, the bright, creative people who work for them, and the suppliers who service them—including the world's leading financial center, which provides the capital that lubricates this huge engine of commerce. The heady mix of writers, agents, editors, publishers, packagers, reviewers, new media, and subsidiary-rights markets like book clubs, newspapers, magazines, merchandising companies, and film producers propels publishing forward in search of the next hot book.

This exhilarating potpourri generates ideas, deals, and an insatiable craving for marketable goods, services, and personalities. Some agents fill their lunch calendars months ahead; others lunch with editors once or twice a week, and still others avoid the ritual altogether, preferring two quiet hours to work.

Lunches and parties help keep agents up-to-date on editors' needs and the latest gossip, and ideas are hatched and deals consummated over the Dover sole. It was at lunch with AAR member Susan Ann Protter that Signet editor in chief Michaela Hamilton, a cat fancier, mentioned that she was looking for a mystery series featuring cats. This was catnip for Lydia Adamson, one of Protter's authors, who as of this writing has twenty-seven mysteries in three series under contract with Dutton/Signet.

However, few agents, if any, make their living over lunch. They make it by phone, by e-mail, snail mail, UPS, Federal Express, and fax machine, and by burning the midnight oil.

During one of our regular trips to New York, a paperback editor was wining and dining us in a chic midtown bistro. We were delighted when she informed us that she wanted to buy a historical romance series and then speechless when she didn't want to negotiate the deal. She refused to talk terms over the Beaujolais and insisted that we wait until she returned to her office and then call her from a phone booth!

Through publishing events and proximity, New York agents enjoy easier access to publishers, the latest news, book and magazine editors, article and book assignments, customers for first-serial sales, publicity media, scouts for foreign publishers and visiting editors, and the New York–based buyers of movie and television rights.

If getting assignments is important to you, you will be better off with a New York agent who is adept at ferreting them out.

However, don't assume that because agents are in the Big Apple they see everyone they need to and know what's going on. As one editor in chief noted, "There are New York agents who are out of it."

Over the years, writers around the country have approached us because they were put off by their impression of the New York publishing world as an impenetrable monolith. They didn't understand the perpetual scramble that agents and editors endure in search of salable books.

We were once talking with a well-established New York agent who said that she had nothing to sell. All of her writers were working on books, so she was sitting around waiting for a book to turn up that she could sell.

Some writers who contact us say that New York agents don't return phone calls. One AAR member who responds to every letter she receives admitted, "I don't return calls from people I don't know unless they are with a publisher, producer, or studio."

However, New York is the most competitive place in the world to be an agent. This means that most agents are at least as anxious as agents elsewhere to find new writers. If you want an agent in New York, stifle your fears and plunge into the fray.

Agents don't work for publishers; they work for writers. So when their publishers are on a distant shore, many writers prefer an agent closer to home. Ability and compatibility matter more than geography.

Life is a series of trade-offs, and although being in New York makes agenting easier, it also makes living harder. New York doesn't start things; it commercializes them. In manufacturing terms, the rest of America is the Research and Development Department; New York is Marketing and Finance. It's the executive suite.

Publishing people go to the same parties, see the same people, read the same media, and live the same urban or suburban lifestyle. This breeds a provincialism that says, "If we don't know about it, it doesn't exist." Until a trend is sanctified by *Time* or the *New York Times*, it doesn't merit recognition.

3.11 Finding the Right Fit: Two Points to Remember

Wherever your search for an agent takes you, keep in mind these enduring truths about the breed:

1. Like editors, agents don't go into the business to get rich. They are agents because they like books and they like people. Publishing is a people business sustained by profit, passion, psychic rewards, and personal relationships.

2. Like writers and editors, publishers and books, agents aren't perfect. Each is a unique blend of strengths and weaknesses. Don't look for perfection. Look for a good fit with your work and your personality.

Happy hunting!

Taking the Vows for Your Working Marriage

The Author-Agency Contract

A verbal agreement ain't worth the paper it's printed on.
–Samuel Goldwyn

In the past, agents preferred handshake agreements. Many still do. But most agents have written contracts. Large agencies have always had them, and movie agents in California are required by law to have them.

Agents who prefer not to have a written contract believe that trust is the foundation of the author-agent relationship. If author and agent trust each other, no written agreement is necessary. If they don't, it's time to get a divorce. New agents often start out feeling this way but then decide to have a written contract to protect themselves, usually after an author has left them without justification.

4.1 *For Butter or for Verse: Covering the Basics*

Some agents supplement their oral understandings with a letter of agreement. Even if your agent doesn't normally use a written contract, he or she should be willing to draw one up and sign it if it's important to you.

Traditional marriage vows commit the bride and groom to stick it out "for better, for worse, for richer, for poorer." To include in a wedding vow everything that can befall a relationship is impossible. For an agency contract to provide for every contingency that can affect a working marriage between an author and an agent is equally impossible.

However, a contract can cover the basics and help avoid misunderstandings that lead to problems. Your contract should spell out the obligations of both you and your agent while the contract lasts and after it ends. It should also describe how you can terminate the contract.

Questions about the author-agent relationship don't arise when all is well. It's only when a real or imagined problem crops up that writers wonder what their obligations are to their agents. One of life's lessons is that you avoid problems by minimizing risks. When your future or large amounts of money may be at stake, do you want to rely solely on your assumptions, your memory, and the goodwill of your agent to protect your interests? A working marriage consummated with a mutually satisfactory contract helps avoid problems and provides the means to solve those that do arise.

Just as no two agents are alike, no two agency agreements are the same. They vary in length, thoroughness, tone, what they cover, and clarity. Some are written in legalese, others as a letter between author and agent.

Your ability to change your agent's contract will depend on your value to the agent and how much the agent wants to represent you. Even if you are a new writer approaching your first agent, you are entitled to a contract that you think is fair. Whatever form your contract takes, you and your agent should reach an understanding on the following points.

4.2   The Confirmation of Your Agent

Unless you and your agent agree otherwise, your agent will expect to have the exclusive right to sell all of your work and your literary services throughout the world. This means that even *you* can't sell your own work; only your agent can. If a publisher asks you to write a book or offers you a contract, you are obligated to refer the publisher to your agent.

One clause may mention the agent's right to hire coagents, specialists who help with subsidiary rights, such as film or foreign rights.

Agents have two big incentives: They want to keep clients, and they want to make money, which they do by placing their clients' work. The contract between you and your agent creates a fiduciary responsibility on your agent's part. Your agent is obligated to act with the highest level of loyalty, fidelity, and good faith in representing you and your work. You have the right to expect honesty, confidentiality, and a professional effort from your agent.

4.3   What Your Agent Will Represent

An agreement can be limited to specific projects or kinds of writing or to a specific territory, such as North America. However, the agent will have the first opportunity to represent or the right of first refusal on all of the client's literary work in all forms: books, plays, screenplays, essays, articles, short stories, and poetry in all print, broadcast, electronic, and merchandising media throughout the world. This includes material that you write or coauthor and that you are commissioned to write. The exceptions to this include work that is already committed to another agent or buyer, writing that you produce as part of your job, and other projects or kinds of writing that you and the agent agree to exclude.

For example, if you are a screenwriter and you already have an agent for your screenplays, the agent you find to sell your novel may agree to exclude screenwriting (and perhaps motion-picture rights to your novels) from the agreement. If your agent wants to represent your novels but you also write poetry, articles, or short stories, which the agent doesn't handle, you should be free to sell them on your own or through another agent.

Because the agent is trying to establish your reputation and may not be making any money in the attempt, or because the agent's efforts have made your other work more salable, the agent may want commissions on work that you sell for yourself or through another agent. You will have to decide whether your agent's efforts on your behalf justify the agent's receiving commissions for work sold without his or her help.

4.4   How Long the Agreement Will Last

Oral or written agreements last only as long as both parties want them to last. Your right to leave your agent is part of the fidiciary relationship. Written contracts may last indefinitely, with the writer given the right to end the agreement with thirty or sixty days' notice. This is, in effect, a one-book contract, because it leaves you free to go elsewhere with your next book.

A contract may state that it lasts for a fixed period of time—one or more years—at the end of which the writer can cancel the agreement or let it be extended automatically for the same period of time. Regardless of what a contract says, however, you may leave your agent at any time.

4.5   The Right to Represent Competitive Books

An agency agreement may include a clause allowing the agent to handle books that compete with yours. Agents vary in their willingness to represent competitive books.

Timing may be the determining factor. If an agent is trying to sell two competitive books at the same time, the agent is faced with the problem of which editors to show which projects to and in what order. The same problem may arise in selling first-serial and subsidiary rights. Also, part of an agent's fiduciary responsibility is to inform clients about potential conflicts of interest.

If one of the books has already been sold or published, handling a second book on the subject may not impair the agent's effectiveness in representing the first book. However, if a second project is clearly competitive with one an agent is already handling, the agent must notify the writers and publishers involved. If both clients are agreeable, the agent should be free to sell the second manuscript.

Certainly, the second author will benefit from the agent's experience with similar books. Publishers who were outbid for the first book may be interested in the second. On the other hand, if an agent has tried unsuccessfully to sell a book like the one you're proposing, the agent may be able to save you time at the outset by telling you to go on to the next project.

In a Peanuts cartoon, Snoopy receives a rejection letter:
Dear Contributor:

Thank you for submitting your story to our magazine. To save time, we are enclosing two rejection slips: one for this story and one for the next one you send us.

4.6   The Commission

This clause specifies your agent's commission, usually 10 or 15 percent. Some agents charge 12.5 percent, and some, if they provide editorial assistance, as much as 25 percent.

If your agent uses a network of foreign agents to handle foreign sales, the contract will specify the foreign agents' commission on such sales, usually 10 percent, which will bring the total commission on foreign sales to 20 to 25 percent. Some agents work through American coagents who charge 20 percent, bringing the total commission to 30 percent. Agents usually split their normal commission with their movie agents but may add 5 to 10 percent for their coagents, bringing the total commission to no higher than 20 percent.

The commission clause may also indicate that commissions earned by the agent do not have to be returned for any reason. Suppose an agent sells a book and receives a commission on the first part of the advance. Then either the author doesn't deliver the manuscript or the publisher decides it's not satisfactory. When the publisher asks the author to return the advance, what should the agent do? Nothing. The agent has done his or her job by selling the manuscript. If the writer doesn't produce, or the manuscript is unsatisfactory, it's not the agent's fault, so why should the agent be penalized by having to return the commission? This is a black-and-white situation.

Other circumstances may not be as simple, however, and regardless of this provision an agent may be willing to return a commission if the author repays an advance and the circumstances warrant it. Some agents take the position that if the writer has acted responsibly, the agent will repay the commission when the writer returns the advance.

4.7   The Agent as Conduit

Your publishing contracts will contain an agent's clause, stating that your agent represents you and enabling your agent to act on your behalf and receive income earned through the contract. The agent deducts a commission, usually 10 or 15 percent, and forwards the balance to you.

Agents who don't have written contracts know that when they sell a book, the publisher's contract will include an agent's clause. Appendix 1 contains sample agents' clauses.

Publishers prefer this system because agents protect them from writers' claiming they never received money due them and because agents serve as knowledgeable mediators if questions arise. As conduits for an author's income, agents are certain to receive commissions.

Agents usually maintain a separate account, so that their clients' income won't be mingled with their own. The money in this account belongs to the agent's clients, not the agency, so if the agency goes bankrupt, the client's income is safe. This standard practice is usually not mentioned in an agency agreement, but you should feel free to confirm it. New agents may not have a separate account because they may not receive enough checks to warrant opening one. State laws about bank accounts also vary.

4.8   Remittance Time

Dorothy Parker once said that the two most beautiful words in the English language are "Check enclosed." The contract should specify how soon your agent will forward your income and royalty statements to you after receiving them. Ten working days is generally enough time for checks to clear in an agent's bank. However, a check in a foreign currency may take months to clear.

4.9   How Expenses Will Be Paid

An agent will pay for local phone calls and ordinary mailing expenses. Your agent may expect you to pay for part or all of the other expenses, such as messengers, long-distance phone calls, faxes, cables, overseas or overnight mailings, photocopying, buying bound galleys and books, and legal advice. An agency contract should indicate what expenses you will pay and when. Regardless of whether it's stated, it's understood that your agent will not commit you to a large expense without your approval.

4.10   Checking the Books

You are legally entitled to examine the entries in your agent's books relating to the income from and expenses for your work. If your agent is absorbing expenses, there will be no need to check them, and there may be no books to check. However, you should receive an itemized list of any expenses deducted from your income. If an agent resists your right to see the financial records being maintained on your behalf, head for the nearest exit. A growing number of agents computerize these records.

If you are receiving royalty statements with your checks, you know the source of the income and how the amount on the check was calculated. At tax time, you will receive a 1099 miscellaneous income tax form listing your gross earnings for the previous year, including your agent's commissions. When you prepare your taxes, you deduct your agent's commissions from your gross earnings.

Just as your agent will, you must always check all of the numbers on your statements carefully, and you must not hesitate to ask about anything that isn't clear to you. You and your agent have an identical interest in making sure that you get every cent you've earned. Ultimately, however, the responsibility for your money is yours.

4.11 Your Freedom to Sign the Agreement

The agency contract should indicate that you are free to sell your work and sign the contract. This protects the agent from conflicts caused by a previous buyer or agent.

4.12 The Right to Assign Income from the Agreement

Your agent does not have the right to transfer you as a client to another agency without your approval if he or she sells out, moves on to something new, becomes ill, or passes away. However, like you, your agent has the right to assign income to others. Agatha Christie assigned the income on her plays and mysteries to her nephew to lessen the burden of inheritance taxes.

4.13 Your Freedom to Assign the Agreement

Although the relationship between a writer and agent ends if either of you dies or is incapacitated, the agreement may state, as a publishing agreement does, that its terms are binding on your heirs or anyone to whom you give the proceeds of the book. Continuing income from authors' estates can be a major source of regular income for agents. Knowing that their literary affairs will be well taken care of after they have crossed the bar can be a source of comfort for writers.

4.14 Which State Law Governs the Agreement

This clause indicates which state's laws will be used to interpret the contract if a dispute arises. Usually, it's the state in which your agent is headquartered.

4.15 Changing the Agreement

Neither you nor your agent can unilaterally change the contract. You must both sign all changes and additions to the agreement, and each of you will have a signed, dated copy.

As your career develops, what you need from an agent may change. Suppose you began as a nonfiction writer and your agreement states that your agent will handle all of your work. Now, however, you want to write children's books, an area in which your agent has no experience or coagents to help. You should be free to sell your children's books yourself or find another agent for them.

If you are selling first-time North American serial rights to short pieces for a one-time payment, the negotiations are much simpler than for a book. You have less need of an agent, especially if you're a freelancer who already knows the editors. Even if your short stories or articles sell for four-figure sums, most agents will be unwilling to handle them because their commissions won't justify the time spent placing them. If agents are earning enough commissions from their clients' books, they may be willing to take care of less profitable work as a courtesy.

Some of Susan Ann Protter's long-term book clients regularly make four-figure sales to major national magazines. They submit their articles themselves but ask Protter to handle the negotiations and make sure that they get paid. If you write short stories or articles and your agent doesn't handle them, ask if your agent will help you on this basis. Large agencies have specialists who sell book excerpts to magazines and may also represent their authors' articles. Agent Andrea Brown, an AAR member who specializes in children's books, represents authors who write many books a year. She encourages them to use their contacts to submit their work. Then the editors call her to make the deals. A short phone call can settle most questions like this.

4.16 When Your Marriage Is Threatened

> The only sure sign that a man is dead is that he is no longer capable of litigation.
>
> –From the *Encyclopaedia Britannica's* entry on death

In case a marital spat does come between you and your agent, your contract should provide a method for resolving it. The simplest way is for you and your agent to agree to discuss the problem, in person or by phone, fax, mail, or e-mail. If you both conscientiously try to solve the problem in a way that is fair to both of you, you may find an equitable solution to the problem. A compromise may be less emotionally and financially costly than a fight.

For a problem that the two of you can't handle, consider these alternatives:

- Use a mediator on whom you and your agent agree. This person can be a judicious, knowledgeable publishing professional or an experienced mediator, whom you find through the publishing, arts, or legal community. A mediator will help you shape a mutually satisfactory solution. This enables both of you to control the outcome.

- Use an arbitrator from an organization that supplies them. The best known of these groups is the American Arbitration Association. Arbitration can be less time-consuming, costly, and technical than litigation, but as with a mediator, the results hinge on how competent and knowledgeable the person is.

- The longest, most painful, and potentially most expensive possibility is litigation. Because anyone can hire a lawyer at any time, this possibility doesn't have to be mentioned in the agreement.

4.17 Getting a Friendly Divorce

You can end your agency relationship at any time. If the time to leave your agent arrives, you won't want to prolong the relationship or slow down the progress of your career. You must make the transition to another agent as quickly and painlessly as possible, so you can get on with selling your work.

The only question is how soon you can leave the agency with a minimum of problems. An agreement with no fixed duration will allow you to end the relationship with a certified letter in a certain period of time, usually thirty or sixty days. This allows time for submissions to be sold or returned and for the agent to notify coagents to wind up their activities. It will also give you time to look for another agent.

If you are between books and your agent or your agent's coagents aren't trying to sell your work, a thirty- or sixty-day waiting period isn't necessary. Send a certified letter saying that you're leaving and the date the termination becomes effective.

If you terminate a contract without cause before it expires, you may be liable for commissions your agent would have earned had the agreement run its course.

4.18 After You Separate

This clause defines your agent's rights and responsibilities after the agreement ends. Agents usually continue to receive their authors' income from sales already concluded. However, if you prefer, your agent can arrange with your publisher to have separate checks and statements sent to both of you.

In any event, your agent has the right to receive the commission on all projects already sold and on those on which negotiations began while the agent represented you.

Just as it is part of your agent's fiduciary responsibility to inform you about all offers, your agent must also, upon request, return manuscripts you have submitted and furnish you with copies of rejection letters. The letters will be helpful if you decide to pursue the sale of your book because you or your next agent will not want to submit your manuscript to an editor who has already rejected it. Chapter 11 discusses ending the agreement.

Another rejection slip for Snoopy:

Dear Contributor:

Thank you for submitting your story. We regret that it does not suit our present needs. If it ever does, we're in trouble.

4.19 Subsidiary-Rights Sales after the Agreement Ends

Another issue to resolve when you leave your agent is the sale of subsidiary rights. If the agent lets the publisher keep all of the book's subsidiary rights, the agent will share in them because the agent continues to receive commissions on contracts that you sign. However, your agent tries to retain subsidiary rights for you. Agents try to sell those rights, and they forward the proceeds from those sales to you as soon as possible.

Agents need subsidiary-rights income to help sustain their agencies. Because your agent made those rights sales possible through the initial sale of your book and then kept those rights out of the publisher's hands for you, he or she may feel entitled to keep representing such rights or to receive commissions on them regardless of who makes the sales. You may save aggravation and money later by clarifying this when you sign up.

The film or foreign rights to a book may be more valuable than the American book sales. Agents make a living by encouraging writers to produce not just one book but many books, with both backlist bookstore and subsidiary-rights potential. This potential may grow over time, as the author's career develops and new possibilities like electronic rights emerge.

If, for example, you become a famous novelist, the foreign and film rights for your previous books may become valuable years later. Winston Groom's *Forrest Gump* made it to the screen twelve years after it was published.

If you've written a nonfiction book that's gone out of print and your agent has had the rights for the book reverted to you, renewed interest in the subject may make it possible to get the book republished.

If you are leaving your agent, your former agent may be willing to split commissions on future deals for rights with your new agent. The trade-off here is that although your first agent will make less money, the income will come in with no effort or expense on that agent's part. Another alternative is to pay two full commissions, which will be worth it if you're receiving a smaller percentage of something rather than a larger percentage of nothing.

On the other hand, even though you've left, your first agent may still want to sell the subsidiary rights for previously sold books. Your new agent is working with some of the same movie and foreign coagents as your first agent, so if trust or ability was not what separated you, there may be no advantage in trying to withdraw subsidiary rights from the first agent. Your and your new agent must decide how to proceed.

4.20   Fie on a Fee

Because no recognized standards exist for agency agreements, no definitive agency contract exists by which you can judge the contract an agent presents to you. You have to be a careful consumer, just as you would when signing any business document.

Your agent should be willing to explain any clauses that are not clear to you and to change the agreement to your mutual satisfaction. If you have concerns about the agreement and the agent isn't willing to discuss them or make changes that you feel are reasonable, research agreements in books, talk to other professionals in your publishing network, check on-line, ask writer's organizations for help, or consider hiring an attorney who knows publishing to go over the agreement with you.

Some agents charge monthly retainer fees to help minimize their risk. If you can afford to subsidize your agent and are otherwise satisfied with the agent's honesty, reputation, experience, and ability, it's up to you to decide whether you want to pay your agent a salary.

4.21   Bills of Writes

Whomever you choose, however the agent operates, and whether your contract with your agent is written or oral, both of you have "certain inalienable rights."

Ken Norwick, a legal counsel for the Association of Authors' Representatives and coauthor of *The Rights of Authors, Artists, and Other Creative People: The Basic ACLU Guide to Author and Artist Rights*, was kind enough to review this book. He noted that these aren't all legal rights, but they are what you and your agent have a reasonable right to expect from each other.

4.21.1 A Writer's Bill of Rights

1. As long as your expectations are realistic, you have a right to be satisfied with what happens to your work.

2. You have the right to approve of how your agent is handling your work.

3. You have the right to expect honesty and professionalism in your agent's relationships with publishers and with you.

4. You have the right to see all correspondence about your work.

5. If your agent declines to handle a project, you have the right to sell it or hire another agent to sell it.

6. If your agent exhausts all of the possibilities for your work and can do no more to sell it, you have the right to take the project back and try to sell it yourself or through another agent, regardless of whether you continue to work with your first agent.

7. You have the right to be informed promptly about all offers for and helpful responses to your work.

8. You have the right to receive prompt replies to your letters and phone calls.

9. You have the right to understand and approve agreements negotiated on your behalf.

10. You have the right to receive income promptly.

11. You have the right to have your business affairs kept confidential.

12. As long as you don't abuse your agent's time, you have the right to ask your agent for news and encouragement.

13. You have the right to have reasonable changes made in your agency agreement at any time.

14. You have the right to stop working with an agent who is not representing you to your satisfaction.

15. If you end your relationship with your agent, you have the right to receive your work back with rejection letters.

4.21.2 An Agent's Bill of Rights

With rights come responsibilities. As you maintain and improve your relationship with your agent, strive to fulfill your obligations.

1. Your agent has the right to work however he or she wishes.

2. Your agent has the right to expect the same degree of professionalism from you that you expect from your agent.

3. Your agent has the right to represent a book that competes with yours, provided that handling the competitive book doesn't lessen the agent's ability to represent your book.

4. If a buyer approaches you about your work or writing services, only your agent has the right to negotiate on your behalf.

5. Except for work that you agree to exclude, your agent has the right to be the only person to represent all of your work for every commercial use.

6. Your agent has the right to continue trying to place a project as long as he or she is competently and conscientiously trying to do so.

7. Your agent has the right to be spared excessive letters, phone calls, and visits.

8. Your agent has the right to be spared requests that are not part of an agent's job.

9. In contracts negotiated for you, your agent has the right to include an agent's clause specifying the commission, the agent's right to receive income and mail for you, and the right to act as agent on your behalf.

10. Your agent has the right not to return earned commissions.

11. If a problem develops between you and your agent, your agent has

the right to discuss it with you and to try to help solve it to your mutual satisfaction.

12. Your agent has the right to stop representing you at any time.

13. If your agent does a good job for you, he or she earns the right to keep you as a client.

14. Your agent has the right to keep his or her home address and phone number private.

4.22 A Modest Proposal

The information in this chapter cannot be the final word, but it will provide a basis for understanding your relationship with your agent, for discussing questions if they arise, and for going your separate ways as painlessly as possible. The author-agent contracts in appendix 2 will give you an idea of what such agreements look like.

If you and your agent trust your instincts, use your common sense, and act in good faith, you will both be doing your part to establish a lasting, satisfying working marriage.

5

Life after Yes

11 Steps to a Happy Working Marriage

> Marriages are made in heaven and consummated on earth.
> —*John Lyly, British writer*

5.1   The Dream Client

Congratulations! You have found an agent who has taken you on and is trying to sell your book. You both are reveling in the honeymoon: the feelings of confidence, enthusiasm, goodwill, and anticipation that follow the consummation of your working marriage.

As with any relationship, the challenge now is to make your working marriage with your agent as fruitful and rewarding as possible. The best way to accomplish this is to be a dream client. What are dream clients? For Elizabeth and me, dream clients are writers who

- Know who we are and approach us in a professional way with fresh ideas, impeccable writing, and enthusiasm

- Are patient, faithful, grateful, creative in coming up with fresh ideas, conscientious about writing and rewriting, and tireless in promoting

- Understand that our working marriage is a collaboration and provide whatever support and ideas they can to help us

- Are totally committed to developing their craft and career

- Deliver a book a year, on time, each book better than the last

- Understand that we want them to be satisfied with our efforts

- Call when they need us

- Mention us in their dedications or acknowledgments

- Become lifelong friends (we need friends more than clients)

- Inspire us to be dream agents

One of the things that makes our list eccentric is what's *not* on it: money. How can you become a dream client?

5.2   Write Well

Make your books as good as they can be. Make your agent, your editor, and your readers eager to see your next book. Also remember that your agent's credibility is on the line with every submission.

A writer sent the manuscript for his novel to a publisher, and on the envelope, he wrote, "FISH INSIDE. DELIVER IN FIVE DAYS OR NEVER MIND."

He got this message back: "PACKAGE DELIVERED IN FIVE DAYS BUT HAD TO OPEN THE WINDOW ANYWAY."

5.3   Deliver Your Books on Time

There are enough challenges in publishing a book. Don't add to them and risk a rejection by being late with your manuscript.

5.4   Communicate Only When Necessary

Bay Area children's book agent Kendra Marcus once faxed a children's book to an editor on a Friday morning and sold it that afternoon. Your book will probably take longer. One point to settle when your agent starts to submit your work is when you can expect to hear from him or her. Unless it's for personal or social reasons such as suggesting an evening out, call or write your agent and expect contact only when it's necessary.

Regardless of how big an author you become, your agent can't devote all of his or her time to you. You may have only one agent, but you are not your agent's only client. Calling your agent about every small frustration will damage your relationship.

However, if you have a serious concern, tell your agent about it immediately. Agents are not mind readers. If a problem arises with your book, your editor, or your publisher that you can't handle, contact your agent. Never assume that your agent knows about the problem, and don't delay, hoping that it will go away by itself.

Don't beat your head against a wall trying to solve a problem by yourself. Part of an agent's value is his or her experience. Your agent may have dealt with a similar problem before and may know how to solve it. He or she may be able to show you why it really isn't a problem or why it's an opportunity in work clothes. Don't be defensive in your relationship with your agent. Remember: You don't work for your agent; your agent works for you.

However, keep in mind that until your agent sells your book, he or she is working for free. When you do contact your agent, be cheerful and optimistic. Ask if there's any way you can help.

5.5   Live and Help Live

When you start working with an agent, agree on how he or she will go about sending out your work and whether one or more copies will be submitted at a time. Once you establish a mutually satisfactory way of working together, be patient. If it stops working, change it.

5.6   Try to Forget about Your Manuscript

Once your agent begins submitting your manuscript, try to put it out of your mind. Publishing is a slow business, and the movement of paper through the labyrinths of the publishing behemoths is slowing down even more. Contracts and advances from large houses used to take one month to arrive, but now they take two months or more.

You and your agent both want to sell your book as quickly as possible, and your agent will be delighted to call you with good news the moment there is any to report. What can you do while you're waiting?

- If you have a brainstorm on how to improve your manuscript and your agent agrees with you, revise it and get it back to the agent quickly.

- If your book isn't finished and you have faith that it will sell, continue to work on it.

- Start your next book.

- Go on vacation.

5.7   *Celebrate When Your Book Is Sold*

When your agent sells your book, show your appreciation. A bottle of champagne or a celebratory meal at a favorite restaurant will do nicely. Publishing people appreciate a simple, relevant gift.

Crown senior editor Peter Ginna feels that personal letters are more meaningful than gifts. The goal isn't to make a grand gesture, just to express your gratitude. For Martha Jane Casselman, the best gifts are a simple thank-you and recommendations to other writers.

5.8   *Acknowledge Your Agent*

Like most people, agents like to see their name in print. Thanking your agent in your dedication or acknowledgments will bring added pride and pleasure every time your agent thinks about your book. When people ask Elizabeth and me if we have children, we say, "No, we have books instead." Your book is your baby, but like you, it's also part of your agent's extended literary family.

5.9   *Promote Your Book*

This essential activity is discussed in chapter 15.

5.10   *Use Your Agent Reflex*

What is an agent reflex (AR)? If an editor approaches you and wants to buy your book or wants you to write one, talk about the book but not about the money. Memorize this line, and use it: "Gee, that sounds great, but if you want to talk about money, you'd better call my agent." Here's hoping you need your AR often.

Even after your book is sold, don't talk to your editor about money without asking your agent. Otherwise, you may do yourself more harm than good.

5.11 Trust Your Agent

Trust your agent to work well on your behalf. You will have the final say about selling your book. Esther Newberg, a senior vice-president at International Creative Management, believes that "it's passion that makes a book work." You might, for example, fare best at a small house or with a small advance but with a passionate editor. Have faith in your agent's instincts as well as your own.

5.12 Be Faithful to Your Agent

Agents take on new writers in the hope that they will become better at their craft and more profitable as clients as time goes by. If your agent gives you a reason to leave, do so without hesitation. However, to leave an agent who is doing an effective job is to deprive the agent of future commissions earned partly because of the agent's commitment to you and your career.

Every book is a book, but every book is different, a unique combination of author, subject, timing, agent, editor, and publisher. Harmonizing these elements to make a book as successful as it can be is a creative challenge for everyone involved. Agents who help their authors do it well earn the right to a lasting relationship.

Mae West once quipped, "Marriage is a great institution, but I'm not ready for an institution." If *you* are ready, be prepared to enter into this secular state with the belief that marriage is not a fifty-fifty proposition. Make it a 100-100 proposition by doing all you can to help it survive and thrive. You and your agent have to be equally committed to doing whatever it takes to create and sustain an enduring relationship.

Part Two

Understanding Your Agent

6

Transforming a Writer into an Author

What an Agent Does before the Sale

> Do you need an agent? No. You don't need an agent. You don't
> need a dentist either. You can fill your own teeth.
>
> > *—James Frey, mystery writer*

> Everyone lives by selling something.
>
> > *—Robert Louis Stevenson*

6.1   *The Recipe for Publishing Success*

An English clergyman once observed that "a baby is a big noise at one end and no sense of responsibility at the other." Your book is your baby. It's something you give birth to, and you want it to be as successful as it can.

You may think that who publishes your first book or how much you get for it is not important as long as it's published. If so, you don't need an agent. It's true that best-sellers and literary classics are rejected, but if your book is good enough, anybody can sell it because any likely publisher will buy it.

The recipe for success in publishing is complex and involves many people. It calls for at least these ingredients: the best possible idea, manuscript, agent, editor, publisher, deal, design, production, sales job by the sales and subsidiary-rights departments, distribution, promotion by the author and the publisher, reviews, bookstore displays, accounting, and luck. These ingredients have to be mixed well and served at just the right time.

Four enduring truths about publishing complicate this recipe:

1. Editors have their own tastes, and publishing houses have their own traditions and personalities.

2. Editors, and the publishers they work for, do certain kinds of books better than others.

3. Although there may be more idealism in publishing than in any other business, editors and publishers vary in their ability and sense of responsibility as much as agents and writers do.

4. You cannot determine whether a publisher will be right for you from its size, its location, or its books. It may, for example, be better for you to have a big book at a little house than a little book at a big house.

How can you acquire three of the most vital ingredients: the best possible editor, publisher, and deal for your book? Enter the literary agent.

6.2   The Agent as Mediator

"What publishers do you work for?" This is a question that probably every agent has heard. Agents don't work for publishers, they work for their clients. They are mediators between two realities: you and the marketplace.

6.3   The Agent as Scout

Agents are the eyes and ears of the publishing business, perpetually on the lookout for new and salable books. Your agent is a scout whose stock-in-trade is knowing what publishers are looking for, which editors can best judge the salability of your work, and which houses can do the best job of publishing it.

6.4   The Agent as Guide

Your agent is also a guide through what may seem to be alien territory. Your agent can explain what you need to know about agenting, publishing, and the craft of writing to help ensure your success. Editors don't have the time to answer all of an author's questions throughout the publication process. Although they, too, are busy, agents work for their writers, so they make time.

There's a cartoon in which a writer exults to a friend, "I just got paid for my manuscript. My agent paid me five dollars to take it someplace else."

6.5   The Agent as Midwife

In *Beyond the Bestseller*, agent Richard Curtis notes that during the paperback boom of the sixties, the role of agents expanded beyond encouraging writers and protecting their interests. Publishers came to depend on agents to help them fill their growing lists.

By reducing the burden on editors to bring in books and develop writers, agents became more powerful by becoming more involved with generating ideas, their clients' writing, and shepherding their clients' books through publication. Before then, books had to be finished before being sold, but agents started selling books on the basis of partial manuscripts, outlines, or even one-page presentations.

Today, your agent is a midwife whose editorial guidance can help you give birth to your idea by turning a loser into a winner. An agent can save you time and frustration by reading your work and judging its salability.

It's tougher than ever to sell the work of new writers to major houses. An agent's advice can make the difference between a manuscript with potential and a successful book. When submissions reach our doorstep, they arrive in one of four conditions:

1. The material is hopeless: Either we don't think it's salable, or it's not right for us.

2. The material is hopeless but the writer isn't, and we ask to see the writer's next book.

3. The material has possibilities, and we discuss with the author how to make it publishable.

4. The manuscript is perfect and ready to send out.

More than 90 percent of the time, it's hopeless. Only once in a plaid moon does a proposal or manuscript reach us ready to submit. Yet unless agents charge for editing, and many do, they don't usually edit an author's work. If writers need help editing their work, we usually recommend freelance editors.

An agent who knows books and publishing can make a world of difference in helping a writer tailor a book to suit publishers' needs. Whether it's a grabbier title, a more marketable angle, a missing element, or smoother prose, by the time an agent sends out a proposal or manuscript, it's stronger and more salable than when it arrived. This is a crucial service because what you receive for your book depends on what editors receive.

A *final rejection for Snoopy*:
Dear Contributor:
  Thank you for not sending us anything lately. It suits our present needs.

6.6   The Agent as Focal Point for Subsidiary Rights

Chapter 4 notes that your agent will expect to handle all of your work in all media throughout the world unless you agree otherwise. As soon as your agent starts to represent your book, he or she will develop a plan for selling subsidiary rights.

One successful agent has a three-pronged approach to selling rights. First he sells the American rights, then the foreign rights, and then he approaches Hollywood. He uses the momentum of one sale to help make the next.

If your book has strong enough subsidiary-rights potential, your agent will start selling them before the book is sold to a publisher. If a property or an author is salable enough, agents can start stirring up interest even before they have a manuscript to sell.

Before and long after publication, your agent follows up on subsidiary rights and sends out information about your book as it becomes available. For subsidiary rights like film and foreign rights, your agent may appoint coagents. Chapter 8 discusses subsidiary rights.

6.7   The Agent as Matchmaker

The relationships between a writer and an agent, editor, and publisher are a series of simultaneous working marriages with personal and professional facets. Your agent is a matchmaker who knows which editors and publishers to submit your project to and, just as important, which to avoid. When your project is ready to be submitted, your agent will discuss with you how best to proceed. Your agent will continue to send out your manuscript until it is sold or as long as the agent feels that he or she can sell it.

Like agents, editors reject more than 90 percent of what they see. A manuscript may be first-rate but unsalable because publishers feel, perhaps wrongly, that it doesn't fit the needs of the marketplace. The book may compete with one of the publisher's current or future books. It may be too early or too late for the book, or it may take the success of the next book to make it salable.

Agents vary in the number of publishers to whom they will submit a manuscript. It depends on how many publishers they deal with, the feedback they receive, how many publishers exist for a book, how much they like it, and their perception of the book's commercial potential. Agents may send out one, two, or three copies of a proposal or manuscript, or as many as thirty copies in a multiple submission.

Some agents will sell a book to any publisher, good or bad; others only to publishers they know will publish a book well. We know an agent who submits manuscripts to just four major houses. If none of them take it, he returns the project. Other agents will keep trying for years.

For a book with strong potential, an agent may conduct an auction, giving publishers a date and ground rules, ranging from simple to complex, for bidding against one another on the project. With the writer's approval, the agent may simply opt for the house that makes the highest bid or may let editors know that various aspects of the deal, including the editor and the house, will be evaluated in determining the best offer for the book.

An editor's skill and passion may be more important than the size of the advance. That's one of the reasons you should visit editors who want to buy your book before accepting an offer, if possible. (Would you marry someone before meeting him or her?) Talking to editors about their vision of your book and its potential, seeing their offices and their books, and meeting other people on the staff is a valuable opportunity to decide if the chemistry is right for your working marriage with an editor and publisher.

6.8   *The Agent as Shock Absorber*

On March 3, 1987, Elizabeth was on the phone negotiating a deal with a small publisher for a first novel. I happened to be nearby, and I started turning the pages of the writer's thick file. When I got to the end of the file, I saw the letter with which the writer had first submitted the manuscript. It was also dated March 3. But it was March 3, 1977. (The novel received a favorable review in the *New York Times*.)

Many books are never sold, despite an agent's best efforts. Rejections can crush a writer (especially ten years' worth), but for agents, absorbing turndowns is just a disagreeable part of the job.

After a series of rejection slips from publishers, Nobel Prize–winning novelist John Steinbeck wrote to a friend, "It is nice to know that so many people are reading my books. That is one way of getting an audience."

6.9   The Agent as Negotiator

When a publisher does make an offer for your book, your agent is a negotiator. He or she hammers out the most favorable possible nuptial agreement for your working marriage with your publisher. When your agent receives the contract, he or she reviews it clause by clause. No contract arrives ready to sign. If your agent is dealing with a publisher for the first time, the contract review usually leads to long letters, faxes, or phone calls discussing changes.

The time it takes to negotiate a contract depends on a combination of factors unique to every sale: the book, the size of the deal, the timing, the people involved, and the house.

The contract for your book is between you and your publisher, so your agent cannot sign it for you. The meaning of a contract's clauses may be obscured by legalese (cynics say intentionally), but with your agent's help, you are the one who must understand, approve, and sign it. You will be responsible for the literary, financial, and legal obligations it contains.

Chapter 8 has more on negotiating.

6.10   Hiring a Literary Lawyer for the Contract

If you place your book yourself, you can hire a literary attorney to help you negotiate the contract. However, lawyers don't read your work, so they can't evaluate an editor, publisher, or offer in relation to better alternatives. That's not their job.

What a literary lawyer can do is go over the contract with you to help get you the most favorable terms and negotiate on your behalf. Before and after contract negotiations, you're on your own. Once the lawyer's hourly fee is paid, you won't have to share your income. Some agents are also lawyers and provide both services.

Volunteer Lawyers for the Arts has enlisted attorneys around the country who will accept reduced fees. For assistance, call (212) 319-2910. Beware: Literary law is a specialty. If you're going to use an attorney, make sure it's someone who knows publishing contracts.

Paper Cuts

A Terrible Day in the Life of an Agent

William Targ, the editor who bought Mario Puzo's *The Godfather* for $5,000 after two editors had turned it down, once remarked, "The trouble with the publishing business is that too many people who have half a mind to write a book do so."

7.1   *If the Moccasin Fits*

"Help me never to judge another until I have walked two weeks in his moccasins." This Sioux prayer may keep you from making an unnecessary mistake in working with your agent. You hired your agent, the agent works for you, and you have the right to be satisfied with what he or she is doing for you. However, you can destroy a salvageable marriage by harboring unrealistic expectations or by misunderstanding your agent's job. Looking at your relationship from your agent's point of view will help you appreciate the agent's problems and concerns. In this chapter and in chapter 10 on a terrific day in an agent's life, you can try my eight-and-a-halfs on for size.

First the agonies. A terrible day in the life of an agent may include any of the following hassles, a composite day-in-the-strife based on real experiences that have happened to Elizabeth and me. They are disguised to protect the guilty. (You know who you are!)

If, as most agents do, you work for yourself, agenting can be isolating. Whether you're in or out of New York, most of your work is done by phone and by mail. There are the writers you represent on one side, the people you sell to on the other, and you in the middle. The people, the phone calls, the paperwork, and the details are endless. If you don't get the endless minutiae right, sooner or later they will come back to haunt you and cost you time, money, clients, and embarrassment.

7.2   The Tuna Moon Crapshoot

I start playing my daily game of telephone tag with editors. The only editor who isn't on another call, not in yet, or at a meeting on this cold, rainy Monday in early spring blithely announces that the deal we negotiated last week is still not definite because it needs the approval of a management committee. An editor usually gets house approval before making an offer. Now I have to tell the author that the deal he and I both thought was firm still has to be approved.

I spill my coffee on a manuscript as I grab the phone for the first call of the day. It's immediately clear that picking up the receiver is my second blunder. In fact, I'm already convinced that my real mistake was getting out of bed.

"What do you mean, you don't feel the vibrations are right for me to represent you?" I ask incredulously after a client says hello to say goodbye.

"Well," she continues with a West Marin airiness, "my moon is rising, and since I was born on the cusp, my astral guide assures me that it would not be good for you to represent me."

What's a star-crossed Capricorn to do? I've been fielding this laid-back Libra's questions for two years while she labored on a how-to so far out I thought it just might be in. Finally, I get to read it, and, shock of shocks, it looks salable. Now, thanks to a rising moon, my hours on the phone and my reading time have come to naught, another fitting portent for a bad day.

One of our coagents in Hollywood calls to report a news flash: A movie one day away from starting production has been scrubbed. *Heaven's Gate* bombed on Friday, our film was killed on Monday. The project, which took more than a year to nudge this far, is as good as dead.

The next call is from a seething client who's had it up to here with the subject of an autobiography on which she's collaborating. She's also angry with me for bringing the two of them together. A minute after I finally put the receiver down, the subject also calls in a royal snit and complains that the writer smokes too much and is dictatorial about how the book should be written and unwilling to make changes because she is "the writer." "Whose story is it, anyway?" she demands to know, thoroughly outraged. It's going to take some heavy three-way palavering to keep this project afloat. I promise both of them I'll get back to them soon, wishing it could be in a decade.

Another marriage made in Helvetica: As if by black magic, the next call is a conference call between two other angry collaborators whose unholy alliance is disintegrating at warp speed. I put together a guy with a story to tell and one of our writers. The guy is unhappy with what the writer is producing. The writer hasn't been able to pull out of the guy what she needs, and she has used up more time than the pittance the guy is fronting for a sample chapter justifies. Both of them feel like they've been taken advantage of, and nothing I can do can make it right for either of them. Fade to black.

Daily two-foot stacks of mail arrive in at least three installments: UPS, package mail, and everything under two pounds in the mail-man's rolling cart. Overnight delivery and messengers also give our doorbell a workout. With a dull thud, the mailman deposits today's hefty stack of morning mail, containing fifteen queries with sample chapters, nine queries without sample chapters, seven rejects, four manuscripts, two proposals, and the usual clump of magazines, bills, and letters.

Eagerly awaiting the arrival of the first bound copies of a promising first novel, I tear open a mailing bag, and sure enough, it's the book. When I open it up, however, pages fall out of it! The bindery screwed up, and I have to hope that the author doesn't become unglued and that this disaster didn't ruin every book in the first printing.

The mail also includes this missive:

Dear Mike:

    Just wanted to let you know that a writer friend put me in touch with Crapshoot Books, who bought my book. What do you think of that? Another friend who's studying accounting took care of the contract. Many thanks for your help.

"Many thanks," he had the chutzpah to write! For the past four months, I read this turkey's manuscript, made extensive suggestions for revision, read a revised version, made further suggestions, read a third version, and sent him our agency agreement, which he never signed. He doesn't even understand that he's taken advantage of my time and that there's no chance I'll be compensated. All I can do is count my blessings and hope that Lady Luck knows she owes me one.

The next call comes from a weeping, frustrated author on the road who has set up an excellent schedule of media appearances, only to find that the books haven't arrived in town yet. They're not even in the bookstore where she's having an autograph party at noon that day. After a heavy dose of verbal TLC and a successful attempt to locate a source of books for the signing, my client is once again ready to smile and continue the struggle up the mountain.

The mail isn't finished with me yet. A note from an editor brings news of this disaster: A beautiful art book I was looking forward to seeing published has been doomed by a typhoon. You may ask how a typhoon can destroy a book. It's easy when it's an art book being printed in Hong Kong. The two-week delay in printing and shipping means that the book won't reach the stores in time for the Christmas rush, which is essential to its success.

After a call from an editor being driven berserk by a client, I dispatch a letter giving the client sixty days' notice. She finds some inconsequential matter that she regards as sufficient reason to badger us at least once or twice a week. Not satisfied with how we were negotiating her contract, she called the editor about it. She's definitely a writer who's better off representing herself.

Still more gloom from the mail pouch: Our agency agreement allows clients to end the agreement with sixty days' notice by registered mail. Signing for a registered letter from a client always causes an uneasy anticipation fulfilled by a writer's saying goodbye. Today is no exception. We tried for three years to sell a science fiction novel for a guy in Montana and finally succeeded, beyond our expectations, because the editor who bought it wanted a series. The series didn't make the author rich, and he decided that his career wasn't moving far enough, fast enough, and it was our fault.

Having opted to take lunch at my desk to stay dry and catch up with the mounting piles of printed matter, I open the next letter as I try to consume a soggy tuna fish sandwich on cold toast. An editor is rejecting the finished manuscript of a specialized how-to book that took twenty-three submissions and more than a year to sell and is unlikely to be sold elsewhere. The reason: Her publishing house has been gobbled up by a larger one with no interest in the subject. The excuse the editor is forced to use is that the illustrations are late. Although there's a chance that we could cajole the house into doing the book, they would kill it with indifference. I am left with the joyless task of informing the author, haggling about repaying the advance, and finding a new home for the book.

I stab myself with a staple as I open a mailing bag sealed with twenty staples instead of the five it requires.

The mail does bring a check. That's good news. The bad news is that the check came about because the numbers on an author's royalty statement made us holler, "Tilt!" and we're still wondering whether the author got all the royalties due him. There's another check, this one postdated! The needy author will be thrilled.

I place a call to the last of ten editors considering a multiple submission and learn that the manuscript is on its way back. It's a how-to book I'm very excited about, and even the editors are returning the project with glowing rejections you could frame, but they just can't get the clods in marketing to agree.

Near the end of the day, I have the depressing task of calling one of our Hollywood agents to let her know that our client has made his choice between the two offers for his book. One was for a small but fair sum from an earnest young producer with no credits; the other for twice as much money from an Oscar-winning director. Our client chose earnestness, which in this case cost him and us money and cost the project the services and credibility of a proven director. Melancholy proof that agents can be only as effective as clients let them be.

My day ends, as most days do, by reading a succession of queries and proposals, all of which have only one virtue: They fail to keep me awake.

To top off this terrible day, the phone wakes me up at five minutes before midnight. Judging from the background noise, it's someone in a bar who sounds utterly sloshed. He wants to know if I would be interested in seeing a best-selling novel he is thinking of writing. I force myself to tell him politely to call back between nine and five.

Since I'm now awake, I decide to take a stab at one last manuscript to try to salvage something from what has been a thoroughly miserable day. Numbed by the inadequacy of what I have endured so far, I start reading . . .

(To be continued in chapter 10.)

The Publishing Contract

Tiptoeing through a Diamond-Studded Minefield

The writer, owing to his temperament, his lack of business training, and his frequent isolation from other members of his profession, is especially unfitted to drive a good bargain with those
who buy his manuscripts.

—Author's League of America pamphlet (1912)

8.1 When an Editor Says Yes

"You know that book we spoke about last week? Well, I brought it up at the
editorial board meeting this morning and got a go-ahead. I'd like to make
you an offer for it." The longer an agent waits to hear those words, the sweeter
they sound. Usually, when an offer is made, the editor has already spoken
to the agent to

- Verify that the book is still available

- Determine whether any other offers have been made on the book

- Let the agent know that the editor is interested, so that if the book
  is being considered by other houses, the agent won't accept another
  offer without first talking to the editor

- Find out what kind of advance the agent is looking for, to make sure
  that it's in the same ballpark as what the editor is thinking about
  offering. (Just as it's essential for you and your agent to share the same
  literary and financial vision of your book, both of you must also accept
  the editor's perspective on the book's potential.)

- Tell the agent when to expect a phone call about the house's decision

8.2　Striking a Deal

> Trust in Allah but tie your camel.
>
> *—Arab proverb*

When the editor calls back, buoyed by the victory of getting the book through the editorial board and eager to make an offer, the discussion will cover the following five topics:

- Your advance

- The payout (how your advance will be paid)

- Your royalties

- Subsidiary rights being withheld for you

- In a hardcover contract, how paperback income will be split

Your agent will also discuss with the editor any issues particular to your book. Depending on how valuable a property you and the book are, this first conversation may also take up special issues such as

- Expense money

- Advance escalators for appearances on the best-seller list

- An advance escalator on a movie sale

- A promotion budget for the book

- Promotion copies

- A first-printing guarantee

The editor covers the essential points of the deal and, depending on the circumstances, may indicate whether there is any flexibility in the numbers. The agent will usually discuss some or all of these points. Then the agent thanks the editor for the offer and promises to respond to the editor after consulting with the author and with any other publishers who have the project.

A contract is a diamond-studded minefield that divides a finite sum of money between two parties. Because contracts are written by publishers, they are loaded with potentially explosive clauses that contain opportunities for your publisher to profit at your expense. Because publishers exist to make a profit, they try to hold on to as much of the money that a contract generates as they can. They do this by trying to hold down advances and royalties, by retaining as many subsidiary rights to a book as they can, by maximizing their share of the income from these rights, by trying to tie down the author's next book, and by including in the contract clauses that benefit them by lowering the author's income.

They can't readily get concessions from their printers or their customers, but for most publishers, an unsuspecting author is always fair game. Simon & Schuster asks for theme-park rights. One publisher has a contract giving themselves world rights for the universe. Now that's thinking ahead! One author admits that she signed a contract offering a $1,000 advance with a 2 percent royalty because "I thought that's what everyone got. I didn't know you could negotiate."

Boilerplates, or publishers' printed contract forms, run from four to more than twenty-eight pages. Their function, once they're filled in with terms, is to establish a mutually satisfactory basis for the publication of your book.

Contracts are an inevitable part of being a successful writer: They protect both parties. However, a contract can be an intimidating document for a new writer. Large houses may have more than one standard contract. We have heard of an editor who used to keep three sets of boilerplates on hand, and whether he's buying a book from a new writer, an experienced writer, or an agent determines which one he pulls out of his desk drawer.

8.3   The Hired Lung: The Agent as Haggler

Negotiating with writers puts editors in a schizophrenic position. When it comes to the book itself, editors and writers share an interest in working together as closely as they can to create the best possible book. Editors want to establish lasting relationships with writers. They know that haggling about money or taking advantage of an author's naïveté will hurt their chances to do so.

Yet editors are paid by publishers, not by writers, and part of what they get paid to do is buy books as cheaply as possible. Responsible editors know that they will be trying to increase their houses' profits at the expense of writers, so they resolve this dilemma by recommending that writers find an agent. Some editors even suggest agents to contact.

Business, like politics, is the art of the possible. The sale of your book will take place or fall through depending on the ability and willingness of your publisher, your agent, and you to agree on a deal. Agents have an obvious interest in wangling as much money as possible out of publishers: The more money their clients make, the bigger their commissions. Here are the points covered in any negotiation.

8.4   Your Advance

"Will you be needing an advance?" a senior editor advises colleagues on what to ask prospective authors after lunch. Why? "You'd be surprised how often they say no."

A first-time author received $2.5 million for his first book based on what one editor called "a thin fifteen-page proposal, much of which was biography." Then he gave it all away to charity. Why would Bill Gates insist on getting $2.5 million and then give it all away? The more they pay, the more they push.

If a large house spends even $100,000 on a book and it fails, they'll write it off as the cost of doing business. They will hope to make it back on the paperback edition or on sales stimulated by future books. If they spend $2.5 million, they have to get behind the book to recoup their investment. Viking spent $1 million promoting *The Road Ahead*. It zoomed to the top of the best-seller list, making Viking's investment a self-fulfilling prophecy.

8.5   The Art of the Possible

The practice of publishers paying authors an advance against anticipated royalties from a book started in the 1870s. Ever since, books have earned income to recoup the advance in two ways:

- Royalties from sales of copies of the book

- Your share of the income from the publisher's licensing of rights to your book and any other commercial uses of the book

Agents can assess the present and future value of a book and an author, but they can't pull rabbits out of hats. New writers often say to us, "Well, since it's my first book, I guess I won't get much money for it, will I?" Probably not, but a publisher will gamble whatever they think your book is worth, regardless of whether it's your first or your fourth. In fact, without a solid track record, it can be *harder* to sell a fourth novel than a first one.

The traditional yardstick for determining advances is the amount of royalties the author will earn on the first printing. In the early forties, the average advance was $500. Now most first-time advances from major houses are in the $5,000 to $25,000 range, but the advance for a genre novel or a literary first novel may be less than that. First-time advances for children's books average $2,500 to $5,000. Little, Brown shelled out $2 million for Alan Folsom's novel *The Day After Tomorrow*. *The Horse Whisperer*, by British screenwriter Nicholas Evans, was sold to Touchstone Pictures for Robert Redford for $3 million. The momentum of this sale led to an auction and a $3.15 million sale to Delacorte. Both of these sales happened before these first novels were even finished. With foreign rights, *The Horse Whisperer* garnered more than $10 million in sales before it was published.

Keep in mind that after you have your advance, you will not receive any more money from your publisher until your book has earned the advance back either through sales of copies or through the licensing of rights. The bigger your advance, the more copies your book will have to sell and the larger the subsidiary rights sales will have to be for the book to earn out.

8.6   *How Your Advance Will Be Paid*

Advances are usually divided into two or more parts, depending on the size of the advance. One common payout is half on signing and half on acceptance of the completed manuscript. In Simon & Schuster's $2 million deal for *Contact*, Carl Sagan's first novel, the advance was spread out evenly over ten years.

8.7   *Your Royalties*

Your royalties will vary according to the format of your book, the discount at which it is being sold, and how and where it is sold. Trade royalties are usually based on the list or cover price of your book. If your book costs $20 and you're earning a royalty of 10 percent, your royalty is $2 per copy.

Specialized publishers and some trade publishers base royalties on the net price of the book, the discounted price they receive for the book. If booksellers buy your $20 book at the standard discount of 40 percent, they pay $12. If your royalty rate is 10 percent of your publisher's net receipts, your royalty is $1.20 per copy.

Here is an overview of hardcover, trade, paperback, and mass-market royalties.

8.7.1 Hardcover Royalties

Although around the turn of the century, hardcover royalties ran as high as 25 percent, they are now usually as follows:

- 10 percent of the list price on the first 5,000 copies sold

- 12.5 percent on the next 5,000 copies

- and 15 percent thereafter

Successful authors command a straight 15 percent royalty or royalties that escalate even higher. Royalties for cookbooks or illustrated books that cost more to design and produce than a book with just straight type may be less.

8.7.2 Trade Paperback Royalties

Royalties vary from publisher to publisher but range from 5 to 10 percent of the list price. A typical royalty scale may start at 6 percent and rise 1 or 1.5 percent after the sale of 10,000 or 20,000 copies. It may escalate again after another sales plateau is reached. A straight 7.5 percent royalty is generally a preferable alternative.

8.7.3 Mass-Market Royalties

Royalties on rack-sized books also vary, running from 4 percent to as high as 22 percent of the cover price for a blockbuster. A royalty of 6 percent on the first 100,000 to 150,000 copies, and 8 percent thereafter, is typical. On books by established authors, agents aim for 10 percent thereafter. The bigger the book, the higher the royalty your agent can demand.

The four defining differences between trade and mass-market paperbacks are size, price, publication, and distribution. Mass-market books come in only one size that fits into the racks in outlets like airports, drugstores, and supermarkets. They have a relatively narrow price range. Trade paperbacks can be any size and any price. Mass-market books were originally sold by independent distributors (IDs), who also sell magazines. So, like magazines, pocket books were published and distributed on a monthly basis. Trade paperbacks, like hardcovers, are published on a seasonal basis. Mass-market paperbacks are sold in 100,000 outlets. Trade paperbacks are sold primarily in 13,000 bookstores.

8.8 Subsidiary Rights

The American Association of Publishers has reported that most trade publishers don't sell enough of their books to make money. For their books to be profitable, they must sell subsidiary rights. The growing importance of subsidiary-rights income to publishers has increased their determination to hold onto whatever rights they can even if they don't know their value or how or when they will exercise them. Agents try to prevent publishers from encroaching on the rights that have traditionally been withheld for writers.

As Martin Levin notes in *Be Your Own Agent*, publishers don't buy books. They acquire the rights to publish books and to serve as the authors' agents in selling subsidiary rights. Your book will have primary and secondary subsidiary rights. Your publisher will expect to control the right to sell primary subsidiary rights for

- Book clubs
- Condensed versions of the book
- Anthologies
- Reprints (if your book is a hardcover) or hardcover publishers (if you're selling to a paperback house)
- Excerpts after publication (this is called second-serial rights)
- Reproduction of part or all of the book without changing it, in all media, including records, films, microfilm, and means of information storage and retrieval

Usually, the only deviation from a fifty-fifty split on these rights is, as described earlier, on the paperback sale.

8.9 Secondary Rights

An agent will try to retain the secondary subsidiary rights:

- First-serial rights (excerpts before publication)

- Foreign rights

- Dramatic rights in all media: film, television, video- and audiocassettes, radio, and theater

- Merchandising rights, also called commercial exploitation, including products such as T-shirts, coffee mugs, calendars, and towels

Your agent will withhold for you all rights not granted to the publisher. The subsidiary rights your agent retains for you may be worth a great deal more than the rights you grant to your publisher. However, they may not become valuable until your work becomes popular or the interest in the subject of your book revives for some unexpected reason, perhaps decades from now. Your agent will stay alert to possibilities for exploiting all rights to your book. Chapter 9 discusses subsidiary rights further.

8.10   The New Wild, Wild West: Electronic Rights

Mark Radcliffe, who with his wife, Dianne Brinson, wrote the *Multimedia Law Handbook: A Practical Guide for Developers and Publishers*, notes that there are three kinds of electronic rights to consider, each of which requires different terms:

- Digital book rights to reproduce the text as is

- Interactive digital rights, including CD-ROMs and software programs

- On-line rights created by work that originates on-line instead of being brought on-line from another medium

CD-ROM rights, which have excited interest in the industry, are closer to dramatic rights than to reproducing the text as is. CD-ROMs involve other media, such as video, audio, graphics, animation, and photography, and therefore they require permissions from other "content providers." The text in books will become only a small part of a CD-ROM.

8.11   The Paperback Split

When a hardcover house sells the paperback reprint rights, the traditional split with the author is fifty-fifty. With sufficient leverage, this can be pushed up in steps to a seventy-thirty split in your favor.

Agent Peter Matson obtained the ultimate paperback split. He sold William Morrow just the hardcover rights to a John Irving novel for $1.3 million, leaving him free to sell the paperback rights separately to Bantam for another $1.3 million.

If circumstances warrant, your agent will request your approval or will at least consult with you on the paperback sale.

8.12   Issues Particular to Your Book

The special issues that contracts can cover are as varied as the writers, editors, and publishers who sign them. For example, if you are signing with a publisher because of an outstanding editor, your agent may try to insert a clause in the contract giving you the right to follow the editor if he or she switches houses before your book goes into production.

8.13   Reaching for the Stars

If your book generates enough interest, your agent may be able to obtain the following clauses for you.

8.13.1 Expense Money

Your agent may be able to get you additional money to cover part or all of your out-of-pocket expenses, such as travel, illustrations, and permissions costs.

8.13.2 Best-Seller Escalator

This escalator and the next one usually only come into play with potential best-sellers. When your book appears on the *New York Times* or *Publishers Weekly* best-seller list, the publisher increases your advance to a fixed ceiling—$50,000, for example—depending on your book's position and longevity on the list. This escalator may also be tied to the sales of the book during a specified period.

8.13.3 Movie Escalator

A movie escalator is a fixed sum, perhaps $25,000, paid when a movie based on your book goes into production.

8.13.4 Promotion Budget

This clause commits the publisher to spend a minimum sum to promote the book.

8.13.5 First Printing

This clause commits the publisher to minimum first printing. Only big books need apply for a contractual commitment to a first printing, and if a book is big enough, the commitment isn't necessary. However, large publishers do base their advances partly on the royalties generated in the first year or by the first printing. Editors estimate the printing and the other deal points in a proposal-to-publish form they have to fill out to persuade the editorial board to buy the book. Your agent will ask about the estimated first printing and cover price to see if your advance is in line with your anticipated royalties.

However, printing estimates are as definite as April weather until shortly before the presses roll. Unless a publisher is committed to force-feeding books into the stores, the first printing of your book will equal the advance sale, or laydown—the number of books the sales reps have gotten into the stores—plus enough additional copies to cover initial reorders.

8.14 Translating from Legalese into Dollars

After discussing the deal with your editor, your agent will go over it with you and discuss any changes that might be possible. Editors usually don't have a great deal of latitude in upping an offer, but your agent will try for whatever improvements you agree are worth a shot.

Even when the terms of the deal are settled, the negotiations are usually not finished. If your agent has already dealt with your publisher before, it is usually possible to use a previous contract—the agent's boilerplate— as a model and just fill in the information pertaining to the new book.

Your agent will check the last contract a client signed with the publisher and negotiate necessary changes.

When it's not possible to use a previous contract as a model, after the foregoing points have been agreed on, the editor sends your agent the filled-in contract so that he or she can review the rest of the clauses. This leads to at least one long phone conversation, perhaps preceded by a fax or letter listing the changes your agent wants. Sometimes someone in the publisher's contracts department goes over the offending clauses with your agent, and they thrash out a contract that is agreeable to both of you.

Some publishers use computers to insert changes in their contracts, so every contract looks made to order. However, most publishers have their contracts printed so they look as if they were carved in stone.

8.15 Thirteen Other Important Contract Clauses

Your contract may contain anywhere from ten to more than a hundred clauses. The most important clauses are these:

- The Grant of Rights

- Copyright

- Delivery of the manuscript

- Approval or consultation on the manuscript, title, and cover

- Revised editions

- The warranty and indemnity clause, which covers your legal responsibilities for your book

- The option clause, which covers one or more future books

- The right to examine the publisher's books

- Author's copies (as many as possible for promotion)

- Obligation to publish in a specified time

- Reversion of rights to you

- Termination of the agreement

- The agent's clause, two samples of which are in appendix 1

Depending on your needs and leverage, your agent may also be able to negotiate for special clauses favorable to you. One example is higher discounts for buying books.

8.16 *Reading between the Lines*

The contract you sign may be far different from the one your agent receives. A publisher's contract may have ironclad clauses that will either take too long to change or that a publisher would rather lose a book over than tamper with. However, most clauses in a contract can be changed if your agent has enough leverage, knowledge, skill, and creativity. The more your publisher wants your book, the more willing they will be to modify the contract in your favor.

At the end of the negotiations, you, your agent, and your publisher must remain enthusiastic about the sale and one another. As throughout the publishing process, your agent helps by serving as a buffer or a lightning rod to absorb problems that arise in working out a satisfactory contract.

Negotiating a contract can take minutes or months. When your agent, your publisher, and, most important of all, you are happy with the results, congratulations are in order. You may have turned a minefield into a gold mine.

9

Following the Money

What an Agent Does after the Sale

There was once a cartoon showing a hulking gorilla saying to a writer: "I realize it's unusual for an agent to charge 75%, but I assure you I'm worth it."

9.1   The Agent as Advocate

The moment your book is sold, you are no longer just another writer. You are an author! Friends in and out of the literary community accord you a larger measure of respect.

Your agent continues to serve as your advocate with your publisher throughout the publishing process. From idea to bookstore, publishing a book usually takes a year and a half to two years. Problems may arise about revisions; a late, rejected, or undelivered manuscript; your editor's leaving the company; the title or cover design; the lack of promotion; or a delayed or faulty royalty statement. Your agent is your advocate and a creative problem solver.

9.2   Deciding When to Sell Subsidiary Rights

Chapter 6 describes what an agent does about selling subsidiary rights before your book is sold. After publication, he or she continues to pursue the sale of any rights to your book that he or she has withheld on your behalf.

Although agents can sometimes solicit interest in or sell subsidiary rights to a project with a proposal or a finished manuscript, unless a book is very timely or commercial, the time to begin is when the manuscript has been accepted and is in its strongest, most salable form. Foreign agents may prefer to wait for bound books.

The two areas that an agent will want to explore as soon as possible are first-serial sales and the book's movie potential. These are discussed in the following two sections.

9.3   Promo Pieces: First-Serial Sales

First-serial sales—getting excerpts into magazines and newspapers before publication—can be a source of income and publicity for you and your book. In general, such sales are more likely for a nonfiction book than a novel because it may be difficult to cut a strong slice from the latter. Your agent may contact magazines, starting with those boasting the highest circulations and first-serial rates, and offer them the right to excerpt your book in one or more article-length excerpts.

Local periodicals may buy your work because you're a local writer. National periodicals will only be interested if the subject will appeal to a large audience. In addition, about 4,000 special-interest magazines—for skiers, car buffs, parents, Internet surfers, photographers, and so forth—always need material. Although they may not pay much, they will reach a receptive audience for your book.

Books from major publishers arrive in stores about a month before publication, later on the West Coast because books are shipped from warehouses in the East. The ideal time for an excerpt to run is at the time of publication, when books are in the stores, so readers who enjoy the excerpt can run right out and buy your book.

Magazines pay more for first-serial sales than for second or post-publication serialization because they have the material exclusively. Different magazines may run different sections of a book concurrently, and the same material may run simultaneously in noncompetitive media, such as newspapers in different cities.

However, first-serial sales are chancy. Magazines are flooded with material, and editors have been known to take an idea submitted to them and assign it to a staff writer or a freelancer with whom they've already worked. They may decide to save money by waiting until after publication or just interviewing the author. Because many first-serial sales are made for less than $1,000, they generate more publicity than income.

In certain situations, it may make more sense for the author to let the publisher license first-serial rights:

- If the book is heavily illustrated, it may be more practical for the publisher to provide the illustrations to magazines.

- If the book is being rushed to press, there may not be enough time to sell excerpts because some magazines have a six-month deadline. Given the shortened production time, a publisher may be better able to meet a magazine's tight deadlines.

- The publisher may have a crackerjack first-serial person.

- A book's first-serial potential may not be large enough to warrant an agent's involvement.

- On big books, publishers may insist on controlling first-serial rights so they can integrate those sales into their overall marketing plan.

The trade-offs: If your publisher keeps first-serial rights, your share of the income may be used to repay the advance. If your agent handles them, your income will be forwarded to you as it's received. Also, although the author usually gets at least 75 percent of a first-serial sale, the split between writer and publisher can range from fifty-fifty to ninety-ten.

If you are a working journalist with connections to newspaper and magazine editors, you may be able to make your own first-serial sales. If so, discuss this with your agent.

9.4   The Big Scream: Going to the Movies

If your book has movie possibilities, your agent will start talking it up to producers, approach a coagent about it, or do both simultaneously, referring leads to the coagent.

We once received a funny, imaginative first novel by Ed Davis about an old dying millionaire who hires a swami to transport her soul into the body of her beautiful young nurse, who will inherit her money. The swami trips, and her soul falls off her penthouse into the body of a drunken bum, leading to humorous complications and a love story with a happy ending.

While we were sending the manuscript to editors, we also started approaching producers with the project. The first producer to see Me Two optioned it. Although we never sold the book—comedies are tough to sell in hardcover or paperback—you can see what Hollywood did with it in the Lily Tomlin–Steve Martin comedy All of Me. At this writing, a musical comedy version is in the works.

Although you don't have to use an agent to sell a book, you *must* have one for TV or movie sales. Studios and producers won't consider unagented material for fear of being sued if they make something similar to a submission they rejected.

Best-sellers are sold in movie auctions for seven-figure sums. Most books, however, are optioned for six months or a year. The option period allows a producer time to get a script written. The script is used to interest actors and a director, obtain financing—perhaps from a studio or from a network if it's a TV movie—and make a distribution deal with a studio if it's to be a feature film. The big payoff comes if the film goes into production.

Nine out of ten options don't get picked up, and even if the one for your book does, a movie is still a long-term proposition. It may take three years or more for a film to go into production and a year to eighteen months more before it's completed and released.

The option price is usually four figures against a five-figure sale price ten times as much—for example, $5,000 against $50,000—if the movie goes into production. Books with strong screen potential will often sell for a five-figure option against a six-figure purchase price—for example, $15,000 against $150,000. An alternative for the sale price is 10 percent of the film's production budget.

You may also get a percentage, usually 2 to 5 percent of the net profits. However, between the real expenses of making, distributing, and promoting a film, and the legendarily tricky Hollywood accounting—sometimes the most creative aspect of a production—your 5 percent will be meaningless unless the movie is another *Jurassic Park. Forrest Gump* made $622 million, but there were still no net profits for Winston Groom. If you can't be a "grosser" and get a piece of the film's gross receipts, the purchase price is all you will receive. In Hollywood, net profits means no profits. However, this is starting to change.

If you're tempted, your agent may be able to get a job for you writing the first draft of the screenplay. This is usually a futile effort predestined for the circular file, so when that happens, don't take it personally. You may also be able to serve as a technical consultant, with or without screen credit, if your expertise will add to the film's authenticity.

Movie interest in a novel may not develop for decades. Your book may have to wait until you're famous, public interest changes, or the right actor, director, or producer reads it and goes wild for it. It took seven decades for Edith Wharton's wonderful novel, *The Age of Innocence*, to make it to the big screen, and look how long it took the Bible.

From the moment your agent starts trying to sell your book as a movie until audiences determine its fate, moviemaking, like the rest of the arts, is an unpredictable endeavor. Unless you are a superstar like Michael Crichton or John Grisham, you will have no control over the process. Time, money, ego, uncertainty, and the craziness that Hollywood generates gave rise to the cliché about how a writer should respond to a movie offer: Take the money and run.

Although some agents sell their own movie rights, the majority work with one or more coagents, most of whom (along with the studios and producers to whom they sell) are in Hollywood. Two trends: Agents are selling books to Hollywood first to build their value, and movie companies are starting their own publishing divisions.

9.5 Foreign Rites

When your book is ready to be sold abroad, your agent will contact his or her counterparts around the world to see if there's any interest in the project. Unfortunately, most books are written in a particular literary and cultural context and don't travel. Brand name authors sell abroad, but most American how-to books on gardening, cooking, sports, and pop psychology won't interest foreign readers.

Solid nonfiction with enduring value—science, history, biographies of world figures, mathematics, technology, business, film, art and illustrated books, and books about big ideas of universal interest—these are among the subjects that will sell. Also salable are books that suit a particular country's tastes and interests. The French and the Japanese love mysteries, and genre romances are popular in many countries. Scandinavians golf in the snow and are eager to learn American techniques. The Japanese are interested in jazz. The Germans and Japanese love science fiction. Books on American culture may do better in English because book buyers interested in them read English.

Top New York agent John Brockman sells directly to foreign publishers, sometimes before approaching American publishers. This helps establish the value for a book and build momentum for the American sale.

Sometimes, the industry "buzz" on a book or a prepublication review in *Publishers Weekly* will spark foreign interest. A successful launch in America or an author's growing popularity over time may also do the trick.

In every country except England, where Charles Dickens had perhaps the first literary agent, the agenting profession is a relatively new phenomenon. In Japan, France, Italy, and Germany, agents sprang up after World War II, when publishers began to acquire American books. Our agency has a network of sixteen coagents covering Great Britain and the Commonwealth, France, the German-speaking countries, Italy, Russia, Eastern Europe, China, Korea, Japan, Holland, Scandinavia, Greece, Israel, Turkey, and the Spanish- and Portuguese-speaking countries. American agents usually split a 20 percent commission, sometimes 15 percent in Britain, with their overseas colleagues.

With illustrated books, publishers may be in a better position than agents to provide foreign houses with the materials they need.

Because of the smaller book and subsidiary-rights markets overseas, advances and royalties for most foreign contracts are smaller than in the United States. Books cost as much abroad, often more than here, and people elsewhere have less discretionary income. Translation costs also affect royalties. In Japan, translators are so important that their names may be more prominent on book covers than the authors'.

9.6 *Views from Abroad*

Our English agent, David Grossman, says, "In many ways, British publishing practice is far more conservative than in the United States, which is a reflection of a society in which the past usually counts for much more than the present or future." This is also true for France and Italy.

William Miller, an agent in Japan, feels that "the agent working in Japan is not merely acting as a business aid to an author, but as a bridge between Japan and the rest of the world over which business can travel."

Ruth Liepman, the founder of the agency in Zurich that represents our German rights, spoke for agents in the United States as well as Germany when she observed, "We get a lot of requests from authors and now and then a top-quality manuscript that makes us all happy. We have not become rich, and I do not think we will ever become rich, but we all work hard, read manuscripts and books, look for good terms, and see to it that the publishers pay."

Nonetheless, best-sellers command hefty advances in major markets, and although they don't usually match American numbers, if your book is sold to half a dozen countries, *mucho dinero* may be heading for your mailbox.

Books, movies, rock, Levi's, television, and the Internet have helped make the international language English and the global culture American. The opening of Eastern Europe and China's acceptance of copyright have opened new markets for American books. It is easier than ever for the right book to change the world. *Crossing the Threshold of Hope* by Pope John Paul II was published simultaneously in twenty-three languages. AAR member Aaron Priest is proud of selling the rights to one of the books he represents to thirty countries.

Philip Roth once said: "Once a book is published, the world edits it." All those solitary months in front of a computer screen will be worthwhile when you start receiving letters from fans around the world.

9.7 The Agent as Lookout

Do words or pictures from your book belong on sheets, T-shirts, coffee mugs, or even toilet paper? If your book sells well enough and has the potential for commercial spin-offs, your agent will investigate merchandising rights. Agents keep an eye out for new rights markets, such as software or CD-ROM rights, that may create possibilities for new subsidiary-rights sales.

Furnishing coagents with what they need—ferrying contracts and other paperwork from where they originate to the writers, figuring out exchange rates for various currencies, keeping track of printings and sales as reported in royalty statements, chasing money from publishers, which can take a tremendous amount of time, and preparing tax forms for writers—requires accuracy, devotion to detail, and time. It simplifies a writer's life to have an agent taking care of these tasks, which produce a steady stream of paperwork.

Litigation can also produce reams of paperwork. If your book causes a lawsuit, your agent may have to testify on your behalf.

Even after writers die, agents help their estates by continuing to act on behalf of their work by selling film, foreign, or other rights, reselling out-of-print books if the opportunity arises, and taking care of royalty payments.

Your agent keeps on top of publishing news and trends and what's going on in the world at large that might create opportunities for you. Because your agent is constantly talking with editors, he or she may be able to obtain writing assignments for you. Agents provide editors with lists of available projects and of clients' interests and backgrounds, which editors can use to find a writer for a project. A creative agent may be able to come up with ideas for you.

An agent may also be able to arrange collaborations between clients with an idea or a story to tell or with the ability to write but in need of an illustrator. If one collaborator is represented by another agent, the agents will coagent the book. Celebrity biographies are often collaborations, sometimes not mentioned, between the subject and a professional hired to do the writing.

Your agent can be a first reader for your work, a sounding board for ideas, and a mentor who helps direct—or, if necessary, redirect—your career. In what may be a desert of rejection, your agent can be an oasis of sympathy and encouragement, a morale booster, and confidant who will help you survive the slings and arrows of personal and literary misfortune.

9.8   Erasing the Line between Client and Friend

Don't expect an agent to be a tax expert, savings and loan, or personal servant. One of the joys of the profession, however, is that enduring friendships do develop between writers and agents that can blur the line of responsibility between duty and affection. Mutual dependencies created by time or success also affect how agents and writers treat each other.

9.9   Six Ways Agents Are Like Publishers

Like publishers, literary agencies are businesses that must make a profit to survive. Agents also have to balance serving the needs of their clients with maintaining their relationships with the publishers to whom they sell. Like publishers, agents

- Are motivated by love or money or both

- Need big books to make big bucks

- Love to get excited about their books and authors

- Must do a good job if they expect to receive a writer's next book

- Start to work with a writer hoping to establish a permanent relationship that will grow more profitable and creative as a writer's career develops.

For most agents, the hardest part of the job is finding good books to sell. If you can write and promote books that meet the needs of the marketplace, the Information Age will be a golden age for you. A literary agent will help you get your share of the gold.

10

Hooked on Books

A Terrific Day in the Life of an Agent

(Continued from chapter 7)

. . . a first novel in the form of letters from a seven-year-old boy to Superman. "Is he kidding?" I think at first. How is he going to bring off a 210-page novel (I always check page length) out of a kid's letters?

By page 20, I'm hooked. By the end of the book, he has made me laugh and cry by using the simplicity of a child's letters to provide insight into sex, God, religion, innocence, love, family, school, growing up, and small-town life. It's a timeless, universal, enthralling novel that will appeal to kids as well as grown-ups.

As I read it, it thrills me to know that I am discovering a major new talent. Also while I read, names of editors who will be right for the book spring to mind unbidden. When I finish the manuscript, I can't wait to share it with Elizabeth and meet the author. (Although it is an adult book, the American Library Association selects it as one of the best books of the year for young adults.)

The discovery of this manuscript in the wee hours of the morning is only the start of a perfect day-in-the-life. It's a glorious spring morning. The sky is clear, the air is crisp, and the sun is turning new leaves brilliant green. After a walk to the waterfront to admire the spectacular beauty of San Francisco Bay, I put on Mozart's "Clarinet Quintet," pick up the paper, and find a glowing review of one of our books, a sign of glad tidings to come.

The day's reading, mail, meetings, and phone calls may yield

- an irresistibly moving, inspiring, and commercial book
- a book that will change the world, or at least improve it
- checks, large and small, for domestic and foreign sales (especially welcome are the checks that I'm not expecting)

- A letter from a new writer or editor who turns out to be a wonderful human being and a first-rate professional

- Calls from new writers who say that an author, agent, editor, bookseller, or reviewer we admire recommended the agency

- A contract negotiation in which we obtain at least some degree of satisfaction on all of the changes we request

- An offer for a book from a good new publisher that exceeds our expectations

- News of a first-serial, foreign, movie, book-club, or seven-figure paperback reprint sale

- A meeting with a writer who has rewritten a proposal exactly as I requested and that I feel certain I'll be able to sell

Our English agent calls to announce that he has just sold the English rights to a novel before the publication date. The author is so pleased that he brings over a bottle of *Dom Perignon* to celebrate.

An editor calls to wrap up a two-day auction that, with escalators, winds up in six figures. I call the author two thousand miles away, and he reports that work on his next book is proceeding beautifully. "You know," he says, "what's the best thing you and Elizabeth have done for me?"

"What?" I ask.

"Your success with my books has given me the freedom to write without having to worry about the rent, and that's the greatest gift you could have given me. I just want you to know that I really appreciate all that you've done for me."

I am delighted that we've helped free him to write, and the kindness of his words makes me misty-eyed. It was a short speech, but it's also Mozart to my ears. Those are sweet words for an agent to hear. He just made my day.

I do not deceive myself into taking an undue share of the credit. His willingness to endure rejections, to hang on for four years until his work gained in popularity, and most of all his ability to write are what won him his freedom. My getting his books to a receptive editor and publisher helped, but ultimately it was the book buyers responding to his gifts as a storyteller who freed him to write.

Agents thrive on a fascinating paradox: Every day is the same, and every day is different. You do the same kinds of things, but each project is a challenge because it involves a unique combination of subject, author, publisher, and timing. The many projects with which you're involved are in different stages of development. There's a constant stream of new ideas and people whizzing by, hoping to interest you. If you are excited by new ideas, it's impossible to stagnate or become bored. The years fly by.

If, as most agents do, you work for yourself, you have the freedom to work in whatever way brings out the best in you and your clients. As soon as your income allows, you can handle only the books that you feel strongly about and can refuse the rest.

Another one of our favorite authors calls. She fulfilled many a Midwest housewife's dream by plunking her typewriter down on her kitchen table and turning out her first historical novel. She's already written twelve books, and is still writing up a storm. She's a warm, delightful lady and it's always a pleasure to hear how she's coming along on her next opus.

The mail brings a two-book contract from a hot new publisher. The covering letter includes the following paragraph:

It is a pleasure to do business with you. The proposals you have provided for my consideration are polished and comprehensive. Your expertise in preparing authors for the publishing process has facilitated my decision-making and acquisitions activity. Additionally, a number of the proposals you represent have very strong market potential. I look forward to our continued communications.

Today's UPS delivery includes an advance copy of a book just off the press. The jacket looks super, and I open the book and see this: "Words would get in the way were I to try to articulate what I feel for Elizabeth Pomada and Michael Larsen who have become much, much more than my agents." This kind of recognition is one of the joys of an agent's life. Only a handful of us get rich from the job, so, like writers, the rest of us need all the psychic rewards we can get. When a writer cares enough about the editorial help you've provided and the two and a half years you've spent selling the book, sustained only by your friendship and conviction, to preface the book like that, you know that, regardless of how well the book does, it was time well spent.

Fortunately, this book became a best-seller, and there are few greater joys in life for either a writer or an agent than seeing your first book on the *New York Times* best-seller list. It justifies your faith in the book, the author, and the publisher's ability to make it work.

Now it's time to meet one of the best editors in the business for one of those long, legendary literary lunches that writers hear about. Despite the three-martini tradition, mineral water is the potable of choice. We both have an afternoon's work ahead of us. By the end of lunch, I feel exhilarated. Once again, I know that despite the hard knocks, the book business is the only way to make a living.

On the basis of what she called "the best proposal I've ever seen," a hardcover editor made a substantial offer for a book. She rides home on the train with a mass-market editor. When I get back from lunch, she calls gleefully to let us know that, six weeks before the book is going to be published, the mass-market editor is so excited about the book that she has made an opening $50,000 offer for the paperback rights.

The mail brings the latest issue of *Publishers Weekly*, which has a very effective ad for one of our books on the cover, the opening shot of a $50,000 promotional campaign.

One of our authors presents seminars on entrepreneurship. I attended one of them and received a list of 555 ways to earn extra money. I took it home, and the next day I thought to myself: "That's a book!" Sure enough, less than two years later, it was. On the acknowledgments page, the author thanked "my high-determination, high-imagination literary agent . . . the person who suggested the book to me in the first place, then coaxed and coddled it to its place in your hands."

A dream client sends the fax she received suggesting changes on her manuscript. It includes these words:

> What a wonderful, wonderful, wonderful book! I had so much fun reading it—the messages come through so beautifully and with such a message of hope. This is truly a book that is going to make the world a better place. What a joy it is to work on! . . . you did a spectacular job on the manuscript and it will be a pleasure to publish.

The widow of an author calls after receiving a royalty check to thank us again for getting her husband's work republished. We were pleased that books of enduring value have a way of surviving neglect.

A call comes from the last of fourteen editors to read what we think is an American classic. When an editor calls and tells you that a manuscript that has been around the block is an American classic, and you've been waiting for more than a year to hear those words, you know you've finally found the right editor. Finding an editor who loves a book as much as you do is guaranteed to send chills up and down your spine. Then the editor backs up her feelings with a solid advance, along with consumer promotion and first-printing commitments. That's my kind of phone call!

Our evening's festivities begin when one of our authors, who has written a book about her adventures as a commercial fisherwoman, arrives with a thirty-pound albacore tuna! She takes one look at our combination of delight and chagrin and, bless her heart, decides that she'd better clean it for us. We feast on the freshest sashimi we've ever tasted. Ah, the joys of living and working in the country's second largest publishing center.

One of our writers is a literary artist who writes six days a week and settles for nothing less than his best work. During dinner, the most delectable course of which is the pleasure of his company, his desire to promote his books and his dedication to writing for posterity as well as for a living illuminate our lives and make for an inspiring evening.

At the end of the day, we go to a sneak preview of a comedy made from one of our books. It's wildly funny. Of course, we are the only people in the theater who cheer during the titles when the phrase "Based on the novel by . . ." flashes on the screen. On the way home from the movies on a beautiful evening, I realize once again that despite its problems, publishing is still the best business to be in.

Although editors and writers want to make a living from their efforts, they are motivated more by ideas, writing, passion, and the transforming power of books than they are by profit. They share the admirable goal of producing books that inform, entertain, inspire, and endure.

New ideas, books, writers, and editors are always enriching our lives, in both senses of the word. It's very fulfilling to be needed and to help talented writers gain the rewards and recognition they deserve.

If you can't write books, the next best thing is helping writers create them by being an agent or an editor. If their books stand the test of time, a little of their immortality rubs off on you.

Imagine making a living reading and buying books (and they're tax-deductible)! I have never met anybody whose job is a better blend of change, beauty, variety, new ideas, pleasure, excitement, the unexpected, challenge, creativity, meeting people, friendship, social value, and stimulation. If you know of one, please let me know.

My faith in the value of life and books, writers, and publishers restored, it's home to hit the manuscript pile again, hoping to find another artist before sleep overtakes me. Yes, agenting is a great business for optimists.

Terminal Transgressions

What to Do When the Honeymoon Is Over

In his memoir *Fun While It Lasted*, Barnaby Conrad remembers "a *New Yorker* cartoon showing a man bending the ear of a bartender: 'When we were first married we were very happy,' he is saying lachrymosely. 'But then as we were leaving the church . . .'"

Marriage is grounds for divorce.

—Sam Levenson

11.1   Seven Potential Problems with Your Agent

The beginning of your working marriage with your agent can be a honeymoon, when everything is fine because you're both on your best behavior. The agent is submitting your book, and you are both eager with anticipation. If the book sells, you're both delighted because it proves that the two of you were right about the book and each other.

If it doesn't sell, the agent's interest may wane. You may realize that although you were right about your book, you were wrong about your agent. This could happen after a month or a year. It could happen with your first book or your twelfth.

As in any marriage, your relationship with your agent will go through a period of adjustment, and you may experience the ups and downs that can befall any continuing relationship. If you both act in a spirit of trust and good faith and have your share of luck, your marriage will have the best chance to succeed.

However, even the most promising marriage can turn sour. The day may come when you decide that your agent is wrong for you, that as someone once said, "Marriage isn't a word; it's a sentence." If that day comes, it's time to think about divorce.

Other than flagrant violations of professional ethics, what reasons justify leaving your agent? The following seven situations indicate that you have a problem.

11.2 Your Agent Never Contacts You

Don't expect an agent to be constantly checking in with you to make sure that everything's okay. However, your agent should inform you promptly about significant developments regarding your work. He or she may only call with good or helpful news, which may be a long time in coming.

At the same time, if you never hear about the progress of your agent's efforts, you may rightly wonder what, if anything, is going on. You can try to avoid this problem by establishing at the outset when your agent will contact you. If your agent repeatedly fails to abide by the arrangement, find out why and change either the system or the agent.

Your agent is not a mind reader. Call or write if you have a question about your work, but don't expect too much in the way of hand-holding, especially until your agent has sold something for you.

11.3 Your Agent Doesn't Answer Letters or Phone Calls

What would you do if your doctor, lawyer, accountant, or anyone else you hired to work for you didn't return your phone calls? You'd hire someone else.

In addition to being a best-selling novelist, Michael Korda is the editor in chief of Simon & Schuster. He qualifies as one of the busiest editors in town, but he returns calls promptly. If he can, anybody can. Agents make their living by mail and by phone. They are extremely sensitive about having their phone calls returned by editors. If your agent wants to represent you, your letters and calls will be answered. If not, hire someone who does.

Trust your agent. Don't become upset if you don't receive an instant response. Find out why. Was the agent ill, very busy, or out of town? A responsible agent will have a satisfactory explanation. If not and poor communication becomes a habit, it's time to move on.

11.4 Your Agent Is Not Actively Pursuing the Sale of Your Work

If your manuscript has become a doorstop in your agent's office, it's not doing either of you any good. Find out what the agent plans to do with the project. Has it been seen by all of the likely editors? If you have an agent who is not in New York, is he or she waiting to discuss the project with editors in person?

Being locked into a long-term contract makes it easier for an agent to be lazy. The agent may figure that no matter what he or she does or fails to do, the writer's not going anywhere.

Once again, agree at the beginning on the best strategy for selling your book, and if that doesn't work and you or your agent can't come up with a second line of attack, you should be free to pursue the sale of the property yourself or seek another agent.

If we temporarily run out of editors to send a project to, we may tell writers to take a shot at selling the book themselves without obligation to us. If they succeed, they can decide then whether they want us to negotiate the contract. Meanwhile, if we find a new editor or imprint, or an editor we know changes houses, or we hear about a house that needs such a book, we will let the author know we are sending it out. Sometimes, a book only needs time and patience to sell.

Just because your book hasn't sold doesn't inevitably mean that you should switch agents. Writing your next book may be the best course. Time spent away from your book may allow the market for it to grow, or you or your agent may come up with a more salable approach to the subject, or the success of your next book may make your unsold work salable.

Agents want to represent authors, not books. They're in it for the long haul. They know that even if a first book doesn't sell, a second one will probably be more likely to, making the rest of an author's books, including previously unsold work, more marketable.

11.5 Your Agent Is Vague about His or Her Activities

If your agent doesn't seem to know what's going on with your book or you're not getting definite answers to questions about your work, find out why. If you're not satisfied, find yourself another agent.

One writer to another:
 "What is your relationship to your agent?"
 "Hand to throat."

11.6   Your Agent Does Not Want to Handle New Work

You've written a book or proposal that you're very excited about, but your agent either doesn't like it or doesn't think much of its chances. If your agent's arguments about the project's weaknesses don't convince you, what should you do? If it happens once, let your agent continue to handle projects under way, and try to find another agent for it or sell it yourself. If your agent continues to reject your work, maybe you should be looking for one who's more in tune with the direction your work is taking.

11.7   Your Agent Is Unable to Sell Your Work

Matching your book with the right time for its publication, the right editor, and the right house may take a phone call or, through no fault of either your book or your agent, years. As long as your agent believes in your book and is trying to sell it, he or she deserves the right to keep trying. However, if it becomes apparent that your agent has run out of houses to submit your book to or no longer cares about it, it's time to separate.

11.8   You Have Outgrown Your Agent

Suppose you are a new writer represented by a small new agency and, to everyone's surprise, your first book takes off and hits the best-seller list. If the book's success is just a fluke unlikely to repeat itself, consider yourself lucky.

However, if you expect to turn out a string of best-sellers, each with strong movie and foreign-rights potential, you may have outgrown your agent. You may decide that you need a larger agency or just an attorney to negotiate contracts. One of the unhappy realities of publishing is the R & D factor: successful writers switching from the small agencies and publishers that develop them to big agencies and publishers. If you have a best-seller, agents will start contacting you. Regardless of your sales, if you feel that your career has developed beyond the point where your agent can represent you well, it's time to move on.

11.9 Two Steps to Freedom

If a problem arises between you and your agent, there are two ways to solve it:

1. Meet with your agent. If that will be too painful, call or write. If your agent has acted conscientiously on your behalf, you owe him or her the opportunity to discuss the problem with you.

   Make sure that your concern is real and justified. If it is, try to find a mutually satisfactory solution to the problem. If you can't, or if after a fair trial, within a mutually agreeable time period, the solution doesn't work, it's time to end the relationship.

   In fairness to your agent, don't approach or commit yourself to a new agent until you've given your present agent a chance to remedy the situation. Ending a basically sound relationship in a moment of perhaps unjustified pique and turning to a second agent who may turn out to be less satisfactory is not a wise decision.

2. Notify your agent of your decision. Your agent's fiduciary relationship with you requires that the agent stop acting on your behalf immediately when you request it. Request it in person or by sending a certified letter explaining the problem and your decision to end your relationship.

   If you meet with the agent, follow up your conversation with a certified letter confirming any new terms you agreed on during your conversation. If you are determined to leave your agent, you can. You may have to consult a literary attorney if your agent offers resistance.

Your agent will continue to be entitled to receive earned commissions and, unless you agree otherwise, checks and royalty statements, and to represent you on the subsidiary rights for the book.

A warning: Publishing is a small world whose denizens thrive on their insatiable appetites for that delectable delicacy, gossip. Avoid becoming known as a difficult author or an agent hopper.

Agents are afraid to drink tomato juice in public because people will think they're drinking their clients' blood.

—Tallulah Bankhead

11.10 Code Makers: The AAR's Code of Ethics

The code of ethics devised by the Association of Authors' Representatives (appendix 3) sets reasonable standards of conduct for agents regardless of whether they are members of the group. If your agent is a member and crosses the line, contact the group. (The address is given in chapter 1.) The AAR's ethics committee may be able to help resolve the situation.

11.11 The Light at the End of the Tunnel

Start looking for a new agent the moment you have notified your first agent that you're leaving. Waiting until you've found a new agent to notify the first one can be embarrassing and can create problems for both agents and for you. That's why some agents won't talk to you until you've severed your previous connection. For instance, what if your first agent gets you an offer for a book and you've just signed an agreement with a second one to handle it?

If your agent gives you a good reason to leave, do what will be best for you personally or professionally. Don't be too concerned about being cut adrift in the literary world. It will be easier to find your second agent than it was to find your first one. However, it's not fair to shop around for a new agent while the first one is still working on your behalf.

Writers also lose agents because the agents die or go out of business. Agents expect to lose clients for a variety of reasons: They've screwed up, they've failed to sell the book, the book is wildly successful, there's no chemistry, the writer is getting a divorce and wants to shed an agent associated with the unhappy past, or the writer acquires a new spouse who doesn't like the agent. The reasons for firing agents—both valid and inexcusable—are endless. One Hollywood agent believed that agents should expect to lose 10 percent of their clients a year, if only because they stop writing or start writing something the agents don't handle.

Every agent who's been in business a while has been contacted by writers who were unhappy with their present agents. That you've had an agent gives you credibility. If you've had a book published, it will be still easier to find a new agent.

12

Why Hire an Agent?

There's an old *New Yorker* cartoon of two men sitting on a couch at a busy cocktail party, having a quiet talk. One man has a beard and looks like a writer. The other seems like a normal person. The writer type is saying to the other, "We're still pretty far apart. I'm looking for a six-figure advance, and they're refusing to read the manuscript."

—From Anne Lamott, Bird by Bird

Except for the unaccountable best-seller, there's nothing mysterious about agenting or publishing, only things you may not know yet. If you're a talented writer, agents and publishers need you more than you need them. You are the reason they exist. This chapter will tell you why an agent can help you and why you need an agent now more than ever.

12.1   Nine Reasons Why an Agent Can Help You

An agent can help you far beyond the immediate goal you share of selling your books. Here's how.

1.   A literary agent is a better judge than a writer of the quality and value of a writer's work and who the best editor and publisher for it might be. There are agents who accept the myth that it's easier to find a publisher than an agent. So they recommend that a writer find a publisher for a book, then hunt for an agent, because an agent will be eager to represent a writer whose book is already sold.

     We've never met a writer who convinced us that he or she had found the best editor and publisher for a book, let alone obtained the best deal for it. You have a right to expect your editor and publisher to act competently and responsibly. However, writers have come to us who regretted signing long, intimidating legal documents that they didn't understand from publishers they didn't know, but they were so eager to get published that they couldn't resist.

Getting a book to the right editor at the right house for the right price can make the difference between success and failure. It can also make the difference between a friendly, creative, profitable experience and pure hell.

A writer once came to us ready to quit writing. His first book had been "privished" (that's the opposite of published) by a small paperback house. He was never able to talk to his editor. He never saw typeset galleys of the manuscript, so he could not respond to the changes that the editor had made. He discovered that the book had been published only when he found it in a bookstore. He couldn't get his royalties. Finally, the publisher went bankrupt, and the author couldn't get the rights to his book back.

In our experience, writers are unable to judge the quality or value of their work, so they don't know if it's as salable as it can be or has to be. Yet writers succeed in selling their books every day of the week. You don't have to have an agent to sell your books. I receive letters from writers around the country telling me how they used my book on proposals to sell their books.

However, writers who can find the best editor and publisher for their work are extremely rare. By finding publishers who will buy their books, all they usually do is prove that their work is salable. Before accepting a deal that a writer brings in, an agent who cares will consider making the proposal or manuscript stronger so it will be worth more and might interest a better publisher.

If you submit your manuscript yourself and a publisher makes an offer, do not discuss terms if you plan to hire an agent to negotiate the deal. You will be tying your agent's hands by accepting an offer before giving him or her a chance to improve it.

A writer asked a critic, "Did you read my last book?"
The critic replied, "I certainly hope so."

---

2.   An agent can teach you what you need to know about publishing to

ensure your success. Editors don't have time to answer all of an author's questions or to provide needed hand-holding during the publication process. Although they, too, are always busy, agents work for their writers, so they make the time to help them.

3. By absorbing rejections and being a focal point for your business dealings, your agent helps free you to write. Because your agent has a fiduciary responsibility to you, you are legally entitled to see all correspondence sent or received on your behalf. However, unless a writer requests them, agents may not forward rejection slips. They don't usually provide helpful information. As with agents, if editors have wasted their time reading something they don't want, why should they waste more time explaining why?

Editors don't always give a real reason, although some editors are more helpful than others in explaining their decisions. If they like a project enough, they'll suggest changes or another editor. In those rare instances in which editors are willing to reconsider a book if the author is willing to change it, they explain what they feel the manuscript needs. Whenever an editor writes anything that can help sell a book, we notify the writer immediately.

My partner, Elizabeth, once submitted a novel to several editors. One wrote back to say that he loved the plot but hated the characters. Another rejected it, saying that she hated the plot but loved the characters. This convinced Elizabeth that all she needed to find was an editor who loved both. She did, but would the writer have been better off enduring the negative reactions that the sale rendered meaningless?

4. Agents are a continuing source of material for editors. As a knowledgeable participant in the publishing process and a valuable source of manuscripts, an agent has more clout than a writer. An author represents only one book to an editor, but an agent represents that book, the author's future books, and the work of all of the agent's other clients, no matter what house the editor migrates to.

5. Your agent may be the only stable element in your career. Your publisher may change hands, and your editor may change jobs. Only your agent will be there throughout your career to assist you in solving the inevitable writing, selling, and publishing problems that arise.

Editors tend to work their way up the pay scale and the editorial ladder by playing musical chairs. Your agent can help start a word-of-mouth campaign going for your book in the trade. Your agent also tries to make sure that the editor's original plans for the book are carried out. This may be a challenge if the editor leaves.

6. Editors at big publishers would rather receive a book from an agent than a writer. Agents know the publishing houses, their lists, editors' personal tastes, and what they need and want. Submissions from agents are better prepared and more professionally submitted than those from writers.

   The traditional route to becoming an editor has been through the slush pile. Secretaries (now called assistants) would wade through stacks of unsolicited manuscripts, hoping to find a diamond in the rough drafts. If they found one, it might become the first book they edited. In the early days of publishing, writers tossed their manuscripts through the transom windows above publishers' doors. Ever since, unsolicited manuscripts are said to arrive "over the transom."

   When Viking published Judith Guest's best-selling novel *Ordinary People* in the early seventies, it was the first over-the-transom book they had published in twenty-six years. Few major publishers now accept unsolicited manuscripts. Before Doubleday stopped reading unsolicited manuscripts, they received 10,000 a year, out of which three or four may have been chosen for publication. Now they and most major publishers rely on agents to screen manuscripts and scout for them.

   Editors at large houses don't have the luxury of time to consider how a potentially salable submission might be improved. They just say yes or no as quickly as they can.

   An agent's credibility is on the line with every submission. If agents submit lemons, editors will ignore the tree that bore them. We encourage editors to stop reading the moment they reach the word that convinces them that a book is not for them, and if that's on page one, that's our problem, not theirs. So it's also in an agent's best interests to submit a project only when it's ready. Crown senior editor Michael Denney guesstimates that it takes editors from two months to a year to read submissions from unagented writers. Editors can't keep agents waiting that long if they want to work with them.

7. Agents have experience in negotiating with editors. Because they understand the give-and-take of negotiating contracts and the economics of publishing, agents can combine realism and their clients' best interests when making a deal. If they've already sold books to

the publisher, they know when editors will have room to maneuver on a deal.

Riverhead executive editor Mary South knows from experience that "agents keep the relationship between editors and authors pure." Editors work for publishers. Their job is to buy books for as little money as possible and to retain as many subsidiary rights as they can for the publisher. This may later poison the relationship between writers and editors and lead writers to switch publishers.

As one editor in chief once noted, "It is not the business of authors and editors to talk about money." Yet the only way editors can avoid taking advantage of writers is to recommend that they get an agent or a lawyer. Editors know that a bitter fight over a contract will hinder their efforts to concentrate on an author's writing. They also know that being fair to a writer helps foster a lasting relationship.

8. Your share of subsidiary rights will usually be greater if your agent, rather than your publisher, handles them. Your publisher will usually apply your share of subsidiary-rights income against your advance, but your agent will forward it to you as it's received.

9. An agent can judge you and your work objectively. Objectivity is an essential asset for an agent. The cliche that a lawyer who represents himself has a fool for a client also applies to writers. When you write a book, you are too close to it to judge its quality or value or to speak on its behalf with objectivity, but your agent can.

For Bantam executive editor Toni Burbank, working with an agent is like having another doctor on a case who can reinforce an editor's (or author's) judgment about a project or a situation or can offer a second opinion.

As a knowledgeable buffer between editor and writer, an agent can temper, interpret, and, if warranted, try to alter editorial and publishing decisions. When authors complain, they are nagging. When agents complain, they're just doing their job.

Agents are only human. They're just as prone to making mistakes as writers, editors, and publishers. They sometimes misjudge books, people, and situations; they may not be available when you need them; their answering machines can screw up; and they're even capable of adding numbers incorrectly. Despite agents' failings, the selling of your book deserves the same kind of knowledge, skill, professionalism, and experience that went into writing it.

A *New Yorker* cartoon entitled "Why the Dinosaurs Perished" shows a dinosaur holding an opened mailing bag and reading from a letter, "Thank you for letting us consider the enclosed manuscript. Although it has obvious merit, we are sorry to say that it does not suit our present needs."

12.2 Five Reasons Why You Need an Agent Now More than Ever

Here are five reasons why you need an agent more than ever:

1. Books have more subsidiary-rights potential than ever, and those rights create responsibilities. Because there are more ways to make money from your books than ever before, you need someone to take charge of

    - Selling rights

    - Negotiating deals

    - Responding to the faxes, phone calls, and paperwork from around the world that selling rights generates

    - Being a knowledgeable, objective advocate on your behalf

    If you want to trade less writing time for greater control over your career, you may be able to sell your books yourself. If you don't mind the trade-off in time and money, your publisher will be happy to act as your agent for subsidiary rights. However, the greater a book's subsidiary-rights potential, the more it will usually cost writers if their publishers, rather than their agents, handle them.

2. The document an editor sees determines what you get. In discussing what agents do for writers, too much emphasis is given to selling the book and negotiating the deal. The fate of almost all proposals and manuscripts is sealed along with the envelope in which they're sent to publishers.

    More than ever, it's essential for an agent to make sure that every submission is as strong as it can be before picking up the phone to find out if editors will read it. Whatever is submitted to an editor has to be right on the money or, regardless of what it's about, it will soon be history.

3. Paperwork is slowing down. The combination of overworked editors and corporate bureaucracies is slowing the rate at which editors respond to submissions, contracts are issued, and checks are dispatched. More than ever, you need someone to follow up on all of the paperwork, including royalty statements, that your book will create.

4. Your house is not your home. In an ideal world, there will be no agents. Writers will write their books as well as they can, publishers will give them whatever the book is worth and spend whatever it takes to make the book successful, editors will take all the time they need to answer all of their writers' questions and work with them for as long as the book needs help. Meanwhile, back to reality. Your editor may be your friend, but your publisher can't be. Major houses are huge, multinational, multimedia conglomerates in which all but a few writers and editors are tiny interchangeable cogs.

   The Chicago gangster Al Capone once warned, "Anyone found sleeping in the trunk of a car deserves to be shot." A writer who approaches a conglomerate without help is asking to be taken advantage of.

   Agents first arose because of publishers' mistreatment of authors. We are once again entering an age of imperial publishing. Best-selling authors will be able to dictate terms, but new and low-selling authors will be forced to submit to publishers trying to grab a larger slice of the larger pie created by new rights and growing markets. More than ever, writers need someone to speak on their behalf.

5. You need someone to track the rapidly changing world of omnimedia. The rate at which publishing, like the rest of civilization, is changing is accelerating. If you want to write, you need someone to keep abreast of what's going on and the certain but unpredictable obstacles and opportunities that lie ahead.

12.3   High Marx

Groucho Marx once said, "We should learn from the mistakes of others. We don't have time to make them all ourselves." A competent literary agent will save you from mistakes that can cost you time and money.

Part Three

The Prequel:
How to Make Yourself Irresistible
to Any Agent or Publisher

The Book Business in a Nutshell

In the 90s, communication and information are entertainment, and if you don't understand that, you're not going to communicate.

—John Naisbitt, best-selling trend mogul

Publishing today is show biz. It's the same as the world of entertainment.

—Irving "Swifty" Lazar, from Swifty: My Life and Good Times

13.1 Controlling Your Career: What You Can Do

It's been said that you can't control the wind, but you can control the sails. You can't control the publishing industry, but you can control your perspective on the business. You can't force people to buy your books, but you can make them want to through your dedication to writing. You can't guarantee your success, but you can be totally committed to your future.

You can make yourself irresistible to *any* agent or publisher if you

- Have a positive but realistic perspective on the book business
- Develop your craft
- Make a 100 percent commitment to your career

Agents appreciate writers who have an understanding of publishing, but what you know about yourself and your goals is far more important than what you know about craft, agents, or the business. Establishing literary and financial goals and making an unshakable commitment to reach them are essential keys to becoming a successful author.

13.2 Y'all Come: America the Theme Park

First, you need to understand the economic and cultural context in which you write, agents sell, and publishers publish. By 2000, the accelerating global electronic convergence of television, the telephone, and computers will create a trillion-dollar business. Two kinds of companies are driving this information revolution: "pipes" companies and "content" companies. Pipes companies provide the hardware and software that transmits information. Content companies create the information and entertainment that whizzes through the pipes: books, articles, music, television shows, films, plays, sports, traditional and electronic games, and on-line services.

To this mix of content, add the endless other ways to sell ideas:

- All kinds of products that range from clothes to toys

- Commercial tie-ins with other companies (McDonald's with its souvenir glasses *du jour*)

- Direct sales through catalogs, retail outlets, and on-line services

What all of this leads to is the realization that the United States is being transformed in part by a major commerce-driven cultural trend: It's becoming a theme park. To understand how effectively all of these elements can be integrated, consider just three empires of commerce: *Star Trek*, *Star Wars*, and Walt Disney. For most Americans, even without children, avoiding their handiwork is impossible. The working marriage of Walt Disney and ABC/Capitol Cities is a prime example of a strategic alliance between a content company and a pipes company.

To place books in the context of what Americans spend on recreation, consider these Department of Commerce statistics for 1994: We spent $370 billion on recreation, but only 6 percent—$22 billion—of that on books and maps. According to one estimate, only 30 percent of the population has ever been in a bookstore. One of the major challenges that publishing faces is not dividing the pie differently but enlarging the size of the pie by increasing the number of book buyers. Let's look at how this need, and the context in which it grows, affects your career.

13.3 Popcorn and Caviar: The Clash for Cash

The nutshell in the title of this chapter refers to the craziness of a business that is subject to the whims of luck, timing, taste, subjectivity, and the economy.

It's been said that in publishing, first you have the writer who can write but can't spell. Then you have the editor who can spell but can't write. Finally you have the publisher who can neither spell nor write, and he makes all the money.

When RCA bought Random House, which it later sold to the Newhouse conglomerate, the accountants were going over Random House's books. At one point, one of them looked up from a ledger with a sudden sense of revelation and exclaimed, "Hey! I got a great idea! Let's just publish the best-sellers!"

When Elizabeth and I worked in publishing in the sixties, the phrase *publishing business* was an oxymoron. You could leave town June 30, return after Labor Day, and not miss a thing. Today, publishing is a year-round business. Back then, frustrated by its inefficiency, people used to ask plain-tively, "Why can't publishing be run like a business?" Their wish has been granted.

Like the rest of the arts, publishing must tread the tightrope between art and commerce. Like writers and agents, publishers want their books published with pride and passion, but to survive, they must publish books that sell.

Independent agent Ned Leavitt has observed that agents' aptitudes and inclinations range from those who are editorially oriented to those who are deal oriented, those primarily interested in words and those primarily inter-ested in dollar signs. Ideally, an agent should be a happy medium between mammon and the muse.

This fundamental tension between art and commerce is captured per-fectly by a *Writer's Digest* cartoon in which an editor reassures an eager young writer by saying, "This is a sensitive, beautifully written story, Ms. Bentley, but don't worry, I'm sure our editors can turn it into a salable property."

Major houses have an appetite for both popcorn and caviar. They want classy books, but must publish the commercial books that support them. An executive vice-president of marketing at Simon & Schuster once explained why: "There are three reasons to publish a book: It will make a profit; the subject is so important it has to be published; or the author shows promise. Without a profit, you can't do the other two."

13.4 Tight Passage: Welcome to the Age of Omnimedia

In *Passages*, Gail Sheehy's best-seller about personal development, she de-scribes passages—periods of struggle and uncertainty—that we must endure as we progress from one stage of life to the next. Right now, publishing is making its way through a passage. Prodded by costs, technology, and the consolidation of different media into competitive, global, omnimedia empires, the publishing business is changing faster and more radically than at any time since it began in England two hundred years ago.

This passage will have profound, irreversible effects on authors and publishing and will help shape the future of media around the world. What happens in the areas of new media marketing, distribution, manufacturing, rising costs, the growing concentration of publishers and booksellers, discounting, copyright, and First Amendment rights will affect your agent, your publisher, and you. Your knowledge of the trends and realities shaping the industry will help you maintain an attitude that balances optimism and realism.

13.5   Publishing by the Numbers

In round numbers, as of this writing, here's a thumbnail sketch of the industry. R. R. Bowker, which publishes *Books in Print* and *Publishers Weekly*, sells a mailing list of 40,000 publishers. More than 3,600 of them publish three or more books a year. Jeff Herman provides information on the 400 most active publishers in his *Insider's Guide*.

Publishers unleash more than 50,000 books a year, about 20,000 of which are trade books that are sold through bookstores. In 1995, the industry generated sales of more than $20 billion by selling more than a billion copies of the 1.5 million titles in print. These include trade, mass-market, religious, professional, mail-order, and university-press books; textbooks; subscription reference series; books sold through book clubs; and new editions of previously published books. Trade books, together with the sales of mass-market books, account for less than half of the industry's sales, and less than half of those books are sold in bookstores.

Although these are impressive numbers, no book, no author, no house, not even trade publishing as a whole is a major factor in the economy. In 1994, the average expenditure on reading material was less than 1 percent of an American family's total expenditures, and it was declining. However, books sales are expected to enjoy healthy growth for the rest of the decade.

13.6   The Urge to Merge: Omnimedia Synergy

A Bob Rogers cartoon in the *Pittsburgh Press* shows an angry man in a bookstore standing at the counter holding a copy of Madonna's photo book,

Sex, and complaining, "This book is nothing but a disgusting, pornographic, shock-value promotional stunt to massage the oversized ego of an exhibitionist superstar. . . . I'll take three." Why is Madonna worth $60 million to Time Warner? Because she's a multimedia conglomerate unto herself: books, movies, television, videos, CDs. Time Warner does them all and so does she. That's synergy.

Tim Allen's unique 1994 "trifecta"—simultaneously having the number one book, movie, and television series—is an example of maximum synergy.

The multibillion-dollar *Star Trek* empire gives added resonance to the word *enterprise*. Pocket Books does the publishing. Paramount does the movies, which are rented and sold by Blockbuster video stores, and the television shows, which are broadcast on United Paramount Network. That's synergy Viacom style.

In what may be a cyclical, century-old pattern, the urge to merge caused a mergermania that is transforming American business. In publishing, the mergers that began in the sixties have created a two-tier industry. The rise of conglomerates on the publishing scene has produced a competitive, glamour industry with better financing and more effective marketing and management.

However, conglomerates have also created a bottom-line mentality that believes in minimizing risk. Media conglomerates are forming a New York–San Francisco–Silicon Valley–Hollywood axis. This union is begetting international strategic alliances (one of the key phrases of the decade and a book idea) between the worlds of film, television, publishing, music, journalism, software, hardware, and cyberspace.

This is the age of the mass-market hardcover, heavily discounted multimillion-copy selling blockbusters by authors like Jean Auel, Michael Crichton, John Grisham, Danielle Steel, Tom Clancy, Robert James Waller, James Redfield, and John Gray.

Reduced overhead and economies of scale make it more profitable for publishers to print and sell 100,000 copies of one book than 10,000 copies of ten books. The advances lavished on the megastars leave less money for new writers who need it.

13.7 80 × 3

AAR member Richard Curtis estimates that mergers have resulted in the loss of 80 percent of the industry's imprints. Seven conglomerates—Bantam Doubleday Dell, HarperCollins, Penguin, Putnam, Random House, Simon & Schuster (S & S), and Time Warner—publish about 80 percent of the books on the best-seller list. Coincidentally, agents supply 80 percent of the books published by major houses. Another symbolic coincidence: The zip codes of all seven publishers start with the same number, 100.

The consolidation in publishing is both horizontal and vertical. Now part of the Viacom-one-come-all conglomerate, Simon & Schuster is the world's largest publisher. The company ships more than 300 million books a year and they generate more than $2 billion a year in sales. S & S is the best example of vertical integration: They publish and distribute in virtually all formats, fields, and media. They do trade adult and children's books, high school and college textbooks, reference books, large-print editions, professional books, direct-mail books, periodicals, training materials, audio- and videocassettes, software, and CD-ROMs.

As mentioned earlier, Viacom and the United Paramount Network (UPN) provide a television connection. Paramount links S & S to the movies, and one of their subsidiaries, Blockbuster, gives them access to video outlets. Viacom has a games subsidiary. They also have an international division with offices in thirty-five countries.

Simon & Schuster President Jonathan Newcomb has a clear vision of the future: "There are two forces driving major change in publishing. One is technology and the other is globalization. . . . We want to be the major technology-driven content provider in the worldwide economy. That's how we are trying to position ourselves." What's your vision of your future?

There is still little or no synergy between the disparate parts of these empires, and some experts doubt that there ever will be. Critics say that synergy is another word for monopoly, but the potential and the desire to take advantage of the possibilities for cross-selling and generating spin-offs remains an irresistible lure.

The growing consolidation of publishers raises the stakes of the publishing gamble, making it harder to sell small books to big publishers. This creates a greater challenge for agents to sell the work of new writers. So if you are a new writer attempting to breach the walls of fortress New York, your book must be impeccable and you must be eager and able to promote it.

13.8 Lunging for the Brass Ring of Best-Sellerdom

Like agents, authors, booksellers, and publishers, books tend to come in two sizes: big and small, best-sellers and everything else. During its short ride on the publishing merry-go-round, your book will have seven chances to grab the brass ring of best-sellerdom. Every house hopes to parlay the momentum generated by

- A big, highly publicized advance
- Intense in-house enthusiasm
- Rave pre-publication reviews in *Publishers Weekly* and *The Kirkus Reviews*
- Huge first-serial, movie, paperback, and book-club sales
- A front-page review in the *New York Times*
- An effective promotion campaign with a promotable author
- "You-gotta-read-this" word-of-mouth recommendations across the country

into a tidal wave of sales on the crest of which a book will surf to the top of the best-seller list.

When *Publishers Weekly* polled people about why they read, they found that the most important reason is pleasure: first the pleasure of reading the book, then the pleasure of touting it to friends. That's why word of mouth alone can make a book successful despite the indifference with which it is published.

HarperPerennial executive editor Hugh Van Dusen admitted that the success of Thomas Moore's first best-seller, *Care of the Soul*, was "a classic example of word of mouth and not traditional publicity."

Simon & Schuster spent $7,500 for another book of spiritual advice by a first-time author. The first printing was 5,000 copies—not an auspicious beginning for a book at a large house. However, word of mouth helped Scott Peck's *The Road Less Travelled* build and maintain the momentum that has kept it on the trade paperback best-seller list for more than twelve years, a remarkable achievement.

13.9 A Hit-or-Miss Business

Publishing is a hit-or-miss, prepublication-oriented business. The first four of the seven chances listed earlier are prenatal influences that occur before publication. If a book hasn't generated momentum by the time the publication date rolls around, the editor and the rest of the house will be too busy thinking about the next list and the list after that to pay attention to it.

The book will either sink or swim, depending on the reception the first printing receives from reviewers and book buyers. Small wonder, then, that according to *Books: The Culture and Commerce of Publishing*, nearly 80 percent of the books published lose money and the only money authors receive from publishers is the advance.

Books was published in 1982, and because big publishers have been pruning their lists, this figure may have changed. However, it will still be less than the 90-percent failure rate for new products in general. In Richard Balkin's excellent book, *A Writer's Guide to Publishing*, he notes that the successful 10 percent of a publisher's fiction list pays for the other 90 percent.

13.10 *Attempting the Impossible: The Perfect Book*

Publishing your book will be a personal, complex, collaborative enterprise. To have the best chance for success, your book should be well edited, copyedited, designed, produced, sold by the sales reps and the subsidiary-rights departments, distributed, promoted, reviewed, and stocked by booksellers.

A multitude of things can go wrong during the publication of a book, and something probably will. To publish a book perfectly is practically impossible.

During one of our spring raids on the Big Apple, during which we see an editor every forty-five minutes, we were in the office of a well-known editor who does serious nonfiction for one of the majors. We were surprised to see on his shelf a mass-market historical romance that the company's paperback division had done. We asked him why it was there.

"Look at the cover," he said.

It was a typical romantic clinch showing a medieval knight kneeling down with his arm around a fair damsel. She had long red hair and a white dress and was sitting in a meadow. After inspecting the cover, we looked at him quizzically.

"Check her hands," he suggested.

We looked again. One hand was clasping her beloved's hand, one hand was leaning on the ground, and there, peeking out from the folds of her dress, was a third hand!

During the inevitable changes that cover art goes through, the artist had been asked to change the position of her hands. But in making the change, the artist forgot to remove the previous appendage. What is unusual is not that the mistake happened, but that the book was published before anyone caught it.

Humorist Sam Levenson once quipped, "Somewhere on earth, a woman is giving birth to a child every ten seconds. She must be found and stopped." Maybe she's the same person who's churning out all the manuscripts that are floating around the ether. Best-selling business author Harvey Mackay estimates that 500,000 manuscripts make their way around the country in a year's time. Only about 10 percent of them are published. However, there are still too many books being published to receive the attention they require from publishers, reviewers, booksellers, or book buyers.

13.11 A Triumph for Travolta

Hardcover publishers have spring and fall lists of books and may also have a third winter or summer list. Mass-market houses have monthly lists. After publishers inform their sales representatives about a new list either at a sales conference or by videocassette, the reps fan out across the country, hawking their wares. Consequently, major New York publishers generally want books of national interest.

Where luck plays a hand is in finding the right editor at the right house at the right time for your book. In addition to having the best possible editor, publisher, and deal, your book must be published at the right time.

One of the most frustrating publishing truths is that regardless of how much or how little a publisher spends to buy or promote a book, it is sometimes impossible to predict how the book will fare in the marketplace. Sometimes, all you need is luck. Here's the story of how the unexpected success of a low-budget rock film resulted in a best-seller. In the spring of 1978, disco dancing exploded in popularity, but word had not yet percolated up to the Big Apple's editorial boardrooms. True to the California tradition of being ahead of its time, Karen Lustgarten's proposal for a disco book had been circulating for more than a year with no takers.

Finally, we didn't sell the book; John Travolta did. A front-page story in the *New York Times* validated the phenomenon caused by *Saturday Night Fever* and the opening of disco-dance palaces around the country. In two weeks, my partner, Elizabeth, placed the book. Warner put it on a crash schedule, sent Lustgarten on a national tour as part of a $50,000 promotion campaign, and *The Complete Guide to Disco Dancing* boogied for almost three months on the *Times* best-seller list.

Another example of timing and luck: After twenty-one years as a Bantam paperback, Maya Angelou's *I Know Why the Caged Bird Sings* hit the top of the *Times* best-seller list and stayed on the list for more than two years at this writing.

13.12 Avoiding Bookicide

Publishers like to avoid risk. As one of our writers once said, "They'll do *anything* as long as it's been done before." Indeed, when one editor in chief was asked what he wanted for his house, he answered, "More of the same only different."

Comedian Fred Allen once said, "Imitation is the sincerest form of television," and so it is with publishing. Agents know that publishers like to jump on bandwagons, but not too early or too late or they land on their financial keisters. When everybody jumps, the result is "bookicide:" Too many publishers pounce on a hot subject, like the arrival of Windows 95, and suffocate it with a barrage of 450 books.

The greater the number of books like yours that have been published, the harder it will be to sell another one. Of course, as best-selling novelist John Saul noted at the Maui Writers Conference, publishers are always prepared to land on either side of the decision to buy a book. "If they don't like a book, they'll say, 'Been done to death.' If they do, they'll say, 'Always works.'"

In 1965, two years before I started working for them, Bantam Books set a world record. From accepting the proposal for *The Pope's Journey in the U.S.* to publication took them just sixty-six and a half hours. By the time *your* book is written, sold, and then produced and distributed by a large house, one and a half to two years will probably pass. An accepted manuscript usually takes nine months to reach the marketplace, the same amount of time it takes to give birth.

13.13 Investing in Authors

Po Bronson gave friends the opportunity to invest in shares of his first novel, *Bombardiers*, which is about selling bonds. The way your proposal or manuscript looks and reads must convince publishers that it's worth the investment that you want them to make in it.

Without including the advance and the cost of printing books, the average investment a major publisher makes in a book is more than $50,000. Trying to hold down advances and royalties and trying to retain rights usually withheld for authors are techniques that publishers employ to help offset their investment.

Agents try to keep as many rights as they can for their authors. Despite the growing value of foreign and electronic rights, publishers don't want to rely on subsidiary-rights sales to justify buying a book. They want their books to earn their keep in bookstores.

13.14 Two Dresses and an Escalator: Publishers in Chains

> Henny Youngman once quipped: "My wife will buy anything marked down. She just bought two dresses and an escalator."

Distribution—getting new books into stores and keeping them there—is a perpetual challenge for publishers. Booksellers and the distributors who sell to them can't stock all of the books that are published. The combined limitations of booksellers' space and budgets force them to return books that don't perform.

The age of the independent bookstore is waning. Independent bookstores are being supplanted by superstores that mark down prices and stock up to 150,000 titles. Bill Shinker, the publisher of Broadway Books, has reported that at major houses, fifteen or sixteen accounts generate up to 85 percent of sales. In some areas of the country, eight chains control 80 percent of the business.

Because booksellers can return unsold books, returns are a perpetual migraine for which publishers have yet to find a cure. Alfred Knopf, who founded the company bearing his name, described this problem succinctly: "Gone today, here tomorrow."

One visionary solution is printing on demand. Someday, you may be able to walk into a bookstore, request a book, and have a copy of it printed on the spot. Despite the problems, more books are available than ever, and it's possible to sell more copies of a book than ever.

13.15 The Spirit of Enterprise: Bottoms Up

The spirit of experimentation and independence is essential for any art to flourish. However, the corporate mentality and high overhead of the publishing behemoths render them less receptive to unconventional ideas and writers without a built-in audience for their work. The opportunity to present new writers and ideas is being seized by small publishers, university presses, and by authors themselves. At the base of the publishing pyramid, computer technology, enterprising writers and publishers, and the censorship of the marketplace have created tens of thousands of small presses and self-publishers, a flourishing cottage industry.

The basic publishing reflex is "I see it. I love it. I publish it." Small publishers still follow where their passions and their low overhead allow them the freedom to go. Nonprofit university presses are also filling the publishing vacuum for less commercial midlist books by becoming more trade oriented.

In between the large and the small publishers are the medium-sized houses that carry on without the benefit of either the resources of the large publishers or the low overhead of the small presses.

13.16 Looking Out for the Competition

> Outside of a dog, a book is man's best friend. Inside of a dog, it's too dark to read.
>
> –Groucho Marx

When it comes to choosing which medium to enjoy, consumers are surrounded by friends. The competition your book will face is enormous. Books are black-and-white in an age of color; columns of type at a time in which visual appeal is an essential element in communications and marketing; and motionless in the age of MTV.

Your book will compete with

- Every idea, proposal, manuscript, and book that agents and editors have read, heard about, accepted, and rejected. That's thousands of books, and the number grows daily.

- Every other book your agent, your editor, your publicist, the sales reps, and the production and subsidiary rights departments are responsible for

- All of the books on your publisher's backlist and all other comparable books

- All of the books published at the same time as yours. Of the approximately 20,000 trade books published a year, the *New York Times* reviews fewer than 2,500 of them, and they review more than any other consumer publication. *Publishers Weekly* reviews about 5,000 books a year.

• All of the other books that distributors and booksellers can stock

• All of the other candidates for subsidiary rights sales. For example, the Book-of-the-Month Club considers 6,000 books a year but selects just 5 percent of them, only 300 books a year.

• Television, movies, newspapers, magazines, newsletters, audio- and videocassettes, software and CD-ROMs, on-line services, and of course television, which TV comedian Ernie Kovacs called a medium "because it is neither rare nor well done." Most of these media are comparably priced or less expensive. Most of them are easier to enjoy, require less time, and are more superficially exciting than books.

• All of the products and services that consumers must buy. Books are purchased with discretionary income, whatever is left over after the basics have been purchased.

Henny Youngman once admitted, "I read about the evils of drinking so I gave up reading." Your book will also compete with all of the other reasons people have to give up reading, and there are more reasons than ever. The competition for people's time is tougher than the competition for their money. If you have never bought a book you didn't read, raise your hand.

In one of Russell Myers' "Broom Hilda" cartoon strips, Broom Hilda is sitting at a typewriter and writes:

Dear Mr. Publisher,
Enclosed is the manuscript for my new novel. It has, I believe, everything necessary to be a bestseller. It weighs 12 pounds, 11 of which are about sex.

Fiction by the pound can still sell, but faster reading time and lower cover prices are behind the trend toward shorter books. Part of the attraction of genre romance novels is that they can be read in a day while the kids are at school.

This list wasn't meant to discourage you but to make you aware of the complex cultural landscape in which you are trying to find happy homes for your books. In the age of omnimedia, the form that information takes is becoming irrelevant. Consumers will buy what they need, depending on price, the information they need, and the most effective way to communicate that information. They will buy a book if they want a biography or a novel, audiocassettes if they're on the road a lot, videos for an exercise program, a CD-ROM for an encyclopedia. Multimedia bookstores are already stocking different media together.

With the right idea, agent, and publisher, competitive media will be a source of income and publicity for you and your books. When you're considering what to write about, try to come up with ideas that you can recycle in as many media as possible.

13.17 Fiction: The Best-Seller Sweepstakes

Agents know that editors love gifted storytellers and are always looking for four kinds of fiction:

- Genre or category books, such as mysteries, Westerns, romances, and science fiction

- Mainstream novels, which have more scope and depth of characterization than genre fiction but are tough to sell when written by newcomers

- Literary novels that are well crafted and character-driven and on which large hardcover houses are reluctant to lose money while waiting for a writer to build an audience

- Best-sellers, which may be genre books with enough heft, scope, and story-telling ability; mainstream or literary novels; or commercial blockbusters

In Elmore Leonard's novel *Get Shorty*, an aspiring writer asks a Hollywood producer what kind of writing makes the most money. The producer replies, "Ransom notes." In publishing, best-sellers make the most money. All houses want them, and in the heat of an auction, large publishers eagerly bid seven figures for them, eight on multibook deals that will keep authors safe from the competition.

George Bosque robbed Brinks of a million dollars, spent it in a year and a half, and then turned himself in. When he was asked how he managed to spend a million dollars in a year and a half, he replied, "Well, I spent half of it on gambling, drink and romance, and I guess I squandered the rest." If publishers believe that they're wagering on the next Michael Crichton or

Danielle Steel, they'll let their competitive spirits seduce them into squandering a bundle in the best-seller sweepstakes.

A struggling writer calls a publisher to ask about a novel she had submitted.

"This is quite well written," admits the editor, "but we only publish work by writers with well-known names."

"Great," shouts the writer. "My name's Smith!"

—10,000 Jokes, Toasts, and Stories

Fiction, more than nonfiction, is a brand-name business, depending on "well-known names." Once authors have paid their dues to join the best-seller club—usually by writing several novels you never heard of before they wrote their breakthrough novels—they have a good shot at a lifetime membership. Most of the novels on the best-seller list are by members of the best-seller club.

The *New York Times* reported that blockbusters are "all but required to keep publishers afloat." Beyond the value of the books themselves, best-sellers are important to publishers because they lead the rest of a publisher's list into the bookstores. At mass-market houses, the top books are even called "leaders."

Stat machine:

- In paperback, fiction outsells nonfiction three to one. The reverse is true in hardcover.

- Women buy 70 percent of the books sold, although it is not known how many they buy for men.

13.18 Nonfiction: Anything Goes

In nonfiction, publishers will take on almost anything for the general public that will sell in bookstores and that ideally has other markets, such as schools and libraries. Nonfiction runs the gamut. There are frontlist humor and novelty books that make a splash and then disappear.

At the other extreme is the philosophy of annuity publishing—that is, reference books and solid how-tos, "evergreens" or backlist books that sell year after year. What's the ultimate backlist book? (Hint: It sells more than 20 million copies a year and the author receives no royalties.)

Publishers are more successful with certain subjects or kinds of books than others. So they tend to stick to the books that they can sell well. This phenomenon is called cluster publishing.

Sandwiched in between the frontlist and backlist books are the midlist books, an endangered species at large houses because, like new fiction by unknown writers, they don't have the potential to be frontlist hits or stable sources of backlist income unless the author's career takes off.

Compared to fiction, nonfiction

- Is easier to write
- Is easier to sell for writers because it can usually be sold on the basis of a proposal instead of the whole manuscript
- Is easier to sell for agents because it's easier to prove the market for a book and the marketability of an author, because more houses publish it, and because agents use multiple submissions
- Is easier to promote
- Has subsidiary-rights potential in more media
- Enjoys a longer shelf life and can often be given a new life with a revised edition
- Is more likely to stay in print
- Lends itself better to talks, seminars, and articles that can be integrated to make a living

This list shows why nonfiction is also a safer bet for publishers. As Avon senior editor Tom Colgan noted, "It's much easier to publish nonfiction." Stat machine:

- About 85 percent of the books published are nonfiction.
- About 75 percent of nonfiction books are by new authors.

13.19 A Format for Every Occasion

Books are being printed in more sizes than ever. Comparable books will suggest whether your book should be published as a hardcover, a mass-market or rack-sized book, or a trade paperback. The price and durability of hardcovers make them principally an information medium, the format for books with lasting value that readers want to keep for reference. A year after publication, 90 percent of successful hardcover books are reprinted in paperback.

Mass-market paperbacks fit into the wire racks you find in supermarkets, airports, and drugstores. The opening salvo of America's paperback revolution was fired in 1939 when Pocket Books published ten 25-cent mass-market paperbacks. In contrast to hardcover books, the mass-market book has for the most part been an entertainment medium, providing classics, genre novels, and best-sellers for readers in search of escape. More than half of the mass-market books published are paperback originals.

Trade paperbacks come in any size, from a small gift book to an 11-by-14 art book or even larger. The Anchor Books imprint at Doubleday, started in 1953, is regarded as the starting point in the history of trade paperbacks, making it the newest of the three formats.

Price and the variety of formats and sizes make trade paperbacks an all-purpose medium, suitable for words and pictures, fiction and nonfiction, the serious and the frivolous, for all stores that sell books and for course adoptions, for reference and for gifts. Trade paperbacks are sold primarily in bookstores. Their lower prices mean that authors receive lower royalties and publishers must sell several times as many copies for the authors to earn the equivalent of the hardcover income.

A book can be published in any combination of these formats, or even, in time, in all three. Publishers do their books in whatever formats work best. Because the major houses do all three, they can control the design, timing, and marketing of each edition.

This flexibility came about because in the mid-sixties, mass-market publishers started publishing paperback originals to avoid the rising cost of hardcover reprints. They also started or acquired hardcover imprints to produce books that could feed their paperback lines. Unable to buy a mass-market house, HarperCollins, Hyperion, Little, Brown, and St. Martin's Press started lines of their own.

The bottom line: When a hardcover house sells the paperback rights to a book, the income is split between the author and the publisher. If your publisher does the hardcover and paperback editions, you receive full royalties.

Rising hardcover prices have made book buyers reluctant to risk their money on new writers, especially novelists. So unless a book has a strong enough hardcover potential, it will be published in paperback. It is less likely to be reviewed but more likely to sell.

Once authors have built a large enough audience or have written a breakout book, the house will start publishing their work in hardcover. Genre fiction, such as romance and mysteries can be a relatively easy way for novelists to break into the business. That's how Janet Dailey and Sue (B-is-for-Best-Seller) Grafton earned their keys to the best-seller club.

13.20 Publishing Goes Global

As if pursuing futurist John Naisbitt's dream of world peace through world trade, the globalization of publishing, along with the rest of the economy is accelerating. This will continue to increase the number of potential readers for your books around the world. There are four signs of globalization:

- The growing number of foreign publishers at the American Booksellers Convention

- The increasing number of foreign-born publishing executives in American houses

- The merging of American and European media companies

- Bantam Doubleday Dell, HarperCollins, Henry Holt, Penguin, St. Martin's Press, and Farrar, Straus & Giroux all being owned by overseas companies

When the movie version of *Like Water for Chocolate* appeared on the *San Francisco Chronicle* best-seller list simultaneously in English and Spanish, it symbolized the beginning of a new era of Spanish-language publishing in *los Estados Unidos*. More than thirty American publishers are doing more bilingual and Spanish editions for the growing Hispanic market.

13.21 A Homage to Your In-House Agent: The Editor as Hero

> The buying policy of this house is the sum of the idiosyncracies of its editors.
> —Hiram Hayden, a former editor in chief of Random House

Of all the publishing realities you need to understand, none is more important to you than how editors work. Once your agent sells your book, your editor will be the first, most immediate, and most vital continuing connection that you will have with your publisher, the nexus between you and everyone else in the house. What roles do editors play?

13.22 Editors Are Publishers with Invisible Imprints

Marc Jaffe, a former editor in chief of Bantam Books, once observed that "a competent editor is a publisher in microcosm, able to initiate and follow a project all the way through." Good editors know how to thrive within publishing's daily, weekly, monthly, seasonal, and yearly cycles and rituals (a book idea).

Editors have to be persistent and creative in ramrodding a book through the stages of publication, which may take years:

- The reading of it

- The lobbying to buy it

- The writing, editing, rewriting

- The copyediting and design of the book

- The sales conference

- The planning and execution of trade and consumer advertising and publicity

- The subsidiary-rights sales

- If it's a hardcover, publication in trade and/or mass-market paperback.

13.23 Editors Are Specialists

Some editors are generalists who will consider anything their houses can publish successfully, but most balance their passions with the house's needs. An agent's stock-in-trade is knowing what kinds of books editors like.

13.24 Editors Are Visionaries

Editors are always write.

−Sign in an editor's office

Editors see not just what a book is, but what it can be. One of an editor's most valuable gifts is the ability to reconcile the writer's vision with the publisher's and the readers' needs.

13.25 Editors Are Subjective Human Beings

An editor is a person who separates the wheat from the chaff and then prints the chaff.

−Adlai Stevenson

French writer André Maurois once quipped: "In literature, as in love, we are astonished at what is chosen by others." Art, like life, is a Rorschach test. Editors see only what they're ready to see at the moment they pick up a manuscript. We've sold books to the third editor at the same house to read them.

13.26 Editors Are Overworked, Underpaid Galley Slaves

In Mark Twain's classic *Life on the Mississippi*, he describes how a riverboat captain knows every changing bend in the 2,000-mile river. He knows where he is all the time, even when he's asleep. Editors, like agents, have to be able to stay afloat while awash in an endless deluge of meetings, phone calls, junk mail, correspondence, books, and other media, jacket proofs, galleys, submissions from agents, memos to others in the house to drum up support for a project, deals, and projects in different stages.

It's been estimated that corporate wage slaves have only six minutes at a stretch to work before they are interrupted. Like agents, editors can't read during the day; they read at night, and on weekends. The perfect title for an editor's autobiography would be *Piles to Go before I Sleep*.

13.27 Editors are In-House Agents

One of an editor's greatest gifts is the ability to be an effective in-house agent for your book. Even though an editor adores your book, that's only the first hurdle. At some houses, editors can simply take a project to their bosses for a decision. Most editors, however, must justify their enthusiasm in three steps. First, they share the book with other editors and key people in the house.

At major houses, editors have to fill out a lengthy computerized profit-and-loss statement, covering a book's contents, markets, the costs to buy and produce it, and its sales, subsidiary-rights, and promotion potential. If the numbers don't prove that the book will make a profit, the editor massages them until they do. Their motto: When all else fails, manipulate the data.

Finally, the editors (or sponsoring editors who speak on their behalf) discuss the book at the weekly editorial board meeting, which includes other editors; members of the sales, publicity, marketing, subsidiary-rights, legal, and design and production departments; and executives of the company—a formidable gauntlet that functions as a devil's advocate for the house.

If anyone on the editorial board can come up with a reason that seems to justify not doing a book, they'll pass on it and go on to the next book. Subjectivity and the group grope for the right decision are two of the reasons why editors turn down manuscripts that become best-sellers.

Because it is far simpler and easier for an editor and an editorial board to say no than yes, your proposal or manuscript must give them as many reasons to say yes as possible and not one reason, not even a bad one, to say no. The more knowledgeable an agent is about a company's key players, the better position the agent is in to influence the decision to buy a book.

13.28 Editors Are the Ultimate Middle People

Editors have to maintain their relationships and continually build new ones with people inside and outside of the house including other people in publishing, trade and consumer media, and domestic and foreign subsidiary rights. One of an editor's greatest challenges is placating both sides of every problem that comes up.

13.29 Hail the Passionate Advocates

Editors who have the courage to take on the powers that be to buy a book, who take the time to edit, who inspire the writers they work with, and who are passionate advocates for their books at every stage of publication inside and outside of the house deserve to be regarded as the heroes of the business. After whoever approves buying your book, your editor will be the most important person in the house in determining the fate of your work. Agents know that a healthy working marriage between you and your editor is an essential key to your success.

13.30 Ya Gotta Have Heart: How Nothing Has Changed

"If we want things to stay as they are, things will have to change."
–*Giuseppe di Lampedusa*, The Leopard, *the beautiful, best-selling novel published posthumously because the only publisher to whom the aristocratic author sent it turned it down*

Less than 400 years ago, Peter Stuyvesant bought Manhattan for the price of a hardcover book. Despite all of the changes transforming the city and the industry since then, there are four reassuring ways in which publishing hasn't changed in the last century:

1. Even with obstacles facing new writers, the industry is remarkably open to new ideas, writers, books, and publishers. Publishing people thrive on passion. If a house believes in a book passionately—because they love it or because they think it will make a profit, or because it simply must be published—they will publish it.

2. The endless supply of excellent editors is an endearing, enduring miracle of publishing. This fountain of youth is one of the ways in which publishing hasn't changed in decades. Although they're condemning themselves to an uncertain tenure at being overworked and underpaid, bright, likable, passionate young English majors continue to attend courses on publishing and then flock to New York in the quest for jobs. There are more dedicated editors in publishing now than ever.

3. Anything is possible. The amazing sales of *The Road Less Travelled*; *The Bridges of Madison County*; *Men Are from Mars, Women Are from Venus*; and *The Celestine Prophecy* continue to prove that books can succeed beyond their authors' imaginations. More than half a century after it was published, the sequel to *Gone with the Wind* catapulted the original back onto the best-seller list both in hardcover and paperback *simultaneously*.

4. Have you ever heard that old country-and-western song "Take Back Your Heart, I Ordered Liver"? Consider the following questions about readers who want heart in their books:

- Why was Amy Tan's *The Joy Luck Club*, a literary first novel about a Chinese family by a Chinese-American, a best-seller and then a hit movie?

- Why did a woman in Marin County, California, buy 60 copies of another first novel, Robert James Waller's *The Bridges of Madison County*, and why did it sell more than 10 million copies around the world?

- Why do category romances account for about half of the mass-market paperbacks sold?

- On the twenty-fifth anniversary of the beginning of her writing career, Danielle Steel finished her sixty-third book on the same 1964 Olympia typewriter on which she wrote the other sixty-two. ("I bought it used for twenty dollars," she recalls, "which was a lot of money for me at the time.") Why is Steel the world's biggest-selling author, with 300 million copies of her books in print?

These books are wildly successful for more than one reason, but what do they all have in common? The mysteries of the heart, an endless source of inspiration. The readers around the world who bought all these books ordered heart.

Every year, the American Booksellers Association gives an ABBY, a book-of-the-year award, for the book that they most enjoyed personally selling to their customers. When Waller won it, he explained his success by saying, "If you write it well enough, they will come." All of these authors "write it well enough" for their readers.

In a superb profile of Jacqueline Susann in the *New Yorker*, S & S editor in chief Michael Korda wrote, "She taught everybody in book publishing that what many people want to read more than anything else is, quite simply, a good story."

For all of the tumultuous changes that the industry is going through, what hasn't changed at all in publishing is that people still need and want to be entertained and enlightened by books with universal themes, whether they're literary, commercial, genre novels, or nonfiction.

13.31 The Power in Publishing: Who's Got It and Why

Where you stand depends on where you sit.
—Miles's *Law of Bureaucracy*

The two biggest chains in the world are invisible. They're the chains that link the writer and the reader, and through the reader other readers, in the transmission of an idea.

Between writer and reader come the gatekeepers: an agent; then all of the staff and freelance specialists who provide services for a publisher: an editor, copyeditor, designer, production director, printer, sales reps, subsidiary-rights people, a publicist, an advertising manager; then, after the book exists: reviewers, distributors, and booksellers. Each link in the publishing chain that comes between your idea and the communication of that idea to readers is either a barrier or a catalyst, depending on the person's competence, receptivity, and perseverance. There are five stages during which control over the fate of a book shifts from the writer to the reader.

The publishing process creates five "power points":

- The first is when you write the book or the proposal for it. You have complete control over the project.

- The second arises if you hire an agent. The agent decides which editors and houses to submit the book to and negotiates the sale.

- The third power point comes as you work with an editor to develop the manuscript. With your editor's help, you determine the final shape of your book.

- The fourth power point occurs when your manuscript is in the hands of the publisher. Now it's the publisher's passion, skill, and creativity in producing and marketing the book that usually determines how it will be received by reviewers, booksellers, and book buyers.

- The last power point is reached when people pick up your book and read it. If they like it enough, regardless of what has happened to the book until then, they will start an invisible book chain of their own by enthusiastically telling everyone they know: "You must read this book!" It's been said that people only die when they are forgotten. Publishers don't keep authors alive; readers do.

That's why, ultimately, the power in publishing comes from authors. Stephen King isn't powerful because he's a nice guy from Maine who plays rock guitar or because he had seven novels rejected before he sold one. King is powerful because, since Doubleday published his first novel, *Carrie*, in 1974, millions of book buyers have paid to read every book he writes.

Aiding the transformation of ideas into books of lasting value is an abiding source of satisfaction for agents. However, as a writer, you are the first and most important link to come between your idea and your readers. How well you develop your idea will determine its reception by the next link in the chain. This also will never change.

13.32 *Spreading Your Wings*

The writing and publishing of your book will be a rite of passage for you. You will go from being someone who thinks you can write a book and have a salable idea to being an author, a potentially life-changing experience.

Once your ideas take flight, they will spread to places and in ways that will surprise and delight you. However, you should venture forth armed with a clear but motivating vision of the brave new whirl you're entering, so you make the most of the extraordinary opportunities that await you.

14

Leaving Out the Parts
That People Skip

How to Make Your Craft Seaworthy

When I want to read a good book, I write one.
–Benjamin Disraeli

I try to leave out the parts that people skip.
–Elmore Leonard

One of the first questions that agents ask themselves about a manuscript as they read it is: How much work will it take to make this manuscript salable? The more work it will take, the less eager they will be to take it on.

Don't submit anything to an agent or editor until it's 100 percent—as well conceived and crafted as you can make it. Make what you submit to an agent create as much excitement as possible. Then it will be easy for you to find an agent and easy for the agent to sell your work.

A book basically offers one of two benefits: Nonfiction provides information; fiction provides entertainment. A book has only two elements: an idea and the execution of that idea. Your job is to generate an idea and execute it so that your book delivers the benefit it promises as compellingly as possible. This takes craft. There are twelve steps you can follow to develop your craft.

14.1 Read

Ernest Gaines, author of *The Autobiography of Miss Jane Pittman*, preaches what he calls "The Six Golden Rules of Writing: "Read, read, read, and write, write, write." He believes that you can only write as well as you read.

Writers always have reasons to read: pleasure, information, inspiration, research. Ray Bradbury recommends that, in addition to learning about all of the arts, writers take half an hour every night and read one poem, one essay, and one short story, both for pleasure and to stoke the fires of the imagination.

If you're a novelist, you should read as many novels as you can, especially those like yours. Become an expert on the kind of book you are writing. What works for you in the books you love will work for your readers. Reading will enable you to learn how to evaluate style and content and assimilate the criteria needed to judge how your work measures up.

Nobel Prize–winning author Toni Morrison once said, "A writer is a reader moved to emulation." Chances are, if books hadn't changed your life, you wouldn't be reading this. Make a list of all of your favorite books, beginning with the first one you can remember, and explain why you love each book. This list is what inspires you to write. In *Bird by Bird*, her marvelous book about writing, Anne Lamott recommends writing a book to "whoever it is who most made you want to write, whose work you most love to read." Read what you love to read, and write what you love to read. Make passion illuminate everything you do. As nineteenth-century art critic John Ruskin declared, "When love and skill work together, expect a masterpiece."

14.2   Learn to Love Words

Playwright Samuel Beckett believed that "words are all we have." Words can inform, enlighten, persuade, motivate, and inspire. They can kill, and they can cure. They can make readers laugh and cry. They can transform people's lives.

Your words will affect your readers in ways impossible to predict or imagine. Every word counts. If there are too many wrong words in a query letter, an agent won't even look at a manuscript.

For a handy set of rules to write and live by, type the list of commandments on composition and style in *The Elements of Style*, an exquisite example of what it advocates, and put it up on the wall where you write. If there's something wrong with your prose, it may well be on that list.

14.3   Understand What Makes Books Work

If you are lucky, you were born with the gift of shaping words so that they sing and ignite sparks in your readers' imaginations. Even if you were born with a gift for writing, however, you were not born with the skill. This you have to learn. Analyze what makes the books you love effective, and you will be on your way to accomplishing your literary goals.

14.4 Get Experience Writing

> In the beginning, clips and contacts, exposure and experience are more important than money, hands down!
> —*Gregg Levoy*, This Business of Writing

There are more ways to make a living as a writer than ever, but any kind of writing experience makes an impression on agents and editors. The longer and more relevant it is to what you're currently writing, the better.

Writing experience will help you develop your skill, it will look good on your resume, and you may be able to use what you learn in your books. Joseph Heller wrote advertising copy for *McCall's* while he was writing *Catch-22*. Before becoming solvent as a writer, Elmore Leonard recalled that "I wrote everything but cocktail napkins to make a living."

E-mail and the on-line services have revived the art of written communication. The world is at your fingertips. Express yourself and develop your professional network at the same time.

Here's something everyone can do every day: Keep a journal. Record your experiences, tribulations, philosophy, ideas, fantasies, snippets of dialogue. A journal can be a confessional, a continuing dialogue with yourself, a means of letting go of thoughts, a valuable resource for your books, a literary autobiography, and raw material for your biographer!

14.5 Come Up with Ideas

> Conception is much more fun than delivery.
> —*Georges Pompidou, President of France*

Because most books are more of the same only different, agents and editors love to find exciting new ideas. Reading books and news media is an inexhaustible source of ideas. One of my favorite *New Yorker* cartoons shows two women nursing cocktails. One is saying to the other, "I'm marrying Marvin. I think there's a book in it." There's a book in just about everything, and there are more subjects to write about than ever.

Willa Cather believed that most of the basic material a writer works with is acquired before the age of fifteen. J. P. Donleavy made a cynical observation along the same lines: "Writing is turning one's worst moments into money." Philip Roth summed up the value of experience to writers when he said, "Nothing bad can happen to a writer. Everything is material."

Brainstorming with your agent and your professional network about subjects that you have already written about or know about can help you find ideas. What topics interest you enough to make you want to research a book about them?

Someone once suggested that if you were going to start a magazine, you should call it *Sex and Money* because that's what everyone wants to read about. Ask yourself, What will America be like in two years? What will its growing, multicultural population need and want to read about? As one editor asked in a more practical vein: "What will people want to save money on two years from now?" Put yourself in the position of a publisher wondering what projects to invest in, and see if your guesses lead to book ideas. Your agent may be willing to brainstorm with you, using these lists of books and ideas to come up with an idea for your next book.

Like your ability to write, your ideas are your stock-in-trade. Keep a notebook or cassette recorder handy so you can make a note of new ideas whenever they hit you. Keep a file for future reference, and don't just limit yourself to book ideas.

Sooner or later, you will also find a use for ideas in scenes, settings, characters, and bits of dialogue, for anything that you think is worth recording. Those alpha-state minutes in the morning and at night, that slow dissolve when you're drifting between being asleep and awake can be among your most creative moments, so be prepared.

Don't suppose that you are the only writer who has hit upon your idea. In our instantaneous, omnimedia twenty-four-hour-a-day environment, we are constantly bombarded with ideas. If one is worth following up, do so as fast as possible without diminishing the quality of your work. However, if your idea is unique and will not soon become dated, take your time. It's far more important that your book be written well rather than written fast.

A publisher will buy your idea in one of two forms: a complete manuscript or a proposal. A first novel usually has to be finished. But if you have proved that you can research and write nonfiction—by selling articles, for instance—a publisher will buy your book on the basis of a proposal consisting of an introduction with fifteen kinds of information about the book and you, a chapter-by-chapter outline, and usually one or two sample chapters. Whether you have an idea, a complete manuscript, or a self-published or out-of-print book, you need a proposal to sell it. Appendix 4 describes the parts of a nonfiction proposal.

One of the joys of being an agent is helping writers develop ideas into salable proposals. Like many agents, I love ideas, and I'm always eager to advise writers after they have read my proposal book but before they start writing. I find that I can always save them time and help them write more salable proposals.

14.6   Research the Subject

Ernest Hemingway believed that you should know ten times as much about a subject as you put into a book. The more you learn, the more you earn. Learning all you can about a topic enriches your writing, makes you more of an authority on the subject, and expands the opportunities to use your knowledge for articles, seminars, publicity, developing subsidiary rights, and other books.

14.7   Outline Your Book

> Every book should have a beginning, a muddle, and an end.
> —*Peter De Vries*

When someone asked Michelangelo why he was chipping away at a block of marble, he replied, "Because there's an angel inside, and I'm trying to get it out." Native American pottery makers believe that the clay will tell them what it wants to be. What your book needs is the best possible embodiment of your idea. So try to make the execution of your idea as strong as the idea itself.

Elmore Leonard doesn't outline his books because, as he said, "I like to be surprised every day." Unless you're a novelist who has to discover what happens as you write, read AAR member Al Zuckerman's *Creating the Blockbuster Novel*. Even if you're not writing a blockbuster, it will help you create the structure for your book that best suits the material. Of course, you should feel free to improve the structure if a better alternative emerges, but when you set out to construct an enduring edifice of prose brick by brick, word by word, give yourself a solid foundation on which to build.

14.8 Establish a Work Style

> All my major works have been written in prison. . . . I would
> recommend prison not only to aspiring writers but aspiring
> politicians, too.
>
> *–Jawaharlal Nehru, Indian statesman*

A popular and sought-after playwright, Edmond Rostand was forced to write
Cyrano de Bergerac in his bathtub because it was the only place in which his
endless callers would leave him in peace. What do you need to write? Do
you write better early in the morning? During the day? At night? Do you have
an office where you can write undisturbed? Mystery writer James Frey guards
his privacy with this sign on his door: "Disturb this writer and die."

Do you use a tape recorder? A typewriter? A computer? Like John Steinbeck,
Ernest Hemingway, Norman Mailer, Joseph Heller, and Alice Walker, Barnaby
Conrad, author of twenty-five books and founder of the Santa Barbara Writer's
Conference, writes with a pen because he feels that any machine gets in the
way of his thoughts and feelings.

Kahlil Gibran once wrote, "Your daily life is your temple and your religion." Write down your daily schedule, putting the hours of the day on the
left side of the page and the activities next to them. If you want to be a
successful writer, you have to pay your dues to the muse by making writing
a daily ritual.

Push yourself with an attainable goal for the number of pages you crank
out a day and a deadline for finishing your projects. A page a day is a book
a year.

There is only one right way to write: in whatever way enables you to
produce your best work. Find the time, place, and writing tools that spur
your best efforts. Sticking to the work style that works for you will boost your
effectiveness, morale, and professionalism. Agents and editors are always
eager to find dedicated word processors.

14.9 Write

Craft leaps off the page instantly. Agents and editors are suckers for good
writing. They will be delighted if, after reading your first paragraph, they can
exclaim to themselves, "At last! This one can really write!"

In reporting on his progress, a writer once told us with an air of confidence, "I've got all the pages numbered. Now all I have to do is fill in the

rest." That's where craft comes in. The prose of pros is an inseparable, indistinguishable blend of poetry and carpentry, art and craft, vision and revision.

One weary editor noted that "you don't have to eat all of an egg to know it's rotten." Every line of your copy must motivate readers to read the next line. The quintessential virtue of salable prose is that it keeps readers turning the pages. If you can keep your readers turning the pages, it doesn't matter what you write about.

The first and last pages of a novel can be vital to its success. Mickey Spillane once said, "The first page sells the book. The last page sells the next book."

When movie producer Samuel Goldwyn was asked what he wanted in a script, he replied that he wanted "a story that starts with an earthquake and works its way up to a climax."

It's been said that the trouble with instant gratification is it takes too long. If you're writing any kind of fiction except literary fiction in the age of computers and MTV, don't keep readers waiting to be entertained. Avoid throat-clearing warm-ups. William Zinsser, the author of *On Writing Well*, recommends that writers hook their readers in the first hundred words. For my partner, Elizabeth: "The story begins when I can't put it down."

Somerset Maugham believed that "to write simply is as difficult as to be good." First-time authors may find it difficult to believe, but when it comes to prose, less is more. Fine writing stands out because of its lack of faults, because authors have the taste to know when a word, sentence, or idea doesn't feel right, and the discipline to revise their work until it does. Effective writing is simple, not unnecessarily flashy; direct, not flowery; concise, with no extra words.

Besides brevity, writing at its best also has passion, vision, and vigor. Bantam executive editor Toni Burbank once remarked about a manuscript, "There was nothing wrong with it, but there was nothing right with it either." As author Cyra McFadden once lamented about another failed effort, "The prose just lay there, dead on the page." Make your writing live for agents and editors. If you have a salable idea, your manuscript will sell. Write as if your future depends on it; it does.

14.10 *Revise*

The writer's best friend is a wastebasket.

–*Isaac Bashevis Singer*

I write the first draft to get the meaning,
The second draft to put in everything I left out,
The third draft to take out what doesn't belong,
And the fourth draft to make it sound like I just thought of it.

–*Margery Allingham, mystery writer*

Think of writing as having two stages. The first challenge isn't getting a book right, it's getting it written. First you have to get something, anything, down on paper, and then you can massage it until it's 100 percent.

Barnaby Conrad, author of *Learning to Write from the Masters* and *The Complete Guide to Writing Fiction*, was once a secretary for Nobel Prize–winning novelist Sinclair Lewis. In Conrad's delightful memoir, *Fun While It Lasted*, Lewis advises him, "Remember, good books aren't written, they're rewritten." Mario Puzo stated it even more simply: "The art of writing is rewriting."

Leo Tolstoy rewrote *War and Peace* seven times. If you read *The Thorn Birds*, part of the reason you enjoyed it is because Colleen McCullough rewrote her thousand-page manuscript ten times (on a typewriter!). Revision is an essential step in producing your best work.

James Joyce understood that "mistakes are the portals of discovery." So bring the spirit of play to your writing. It's been said that you should "never consider yourself a failure. You can always serve as a bad example." Let the chance to revise your work as often as necessary liberate your creativity. Let your imagination soar in early drafts, knowing that craft will assert itself later. Only your last revision counts, that final reckoning when you must resolve the tension between thought and feeling and make every word count.

In a cartoon in *Books, Books, Books*, there are two mice on a writer's desk in the middle of the night, reading a manuscript. One mouse says to the other, "We'd do him a big favor if we ate chapter four." If you don't want to risk rodents criticizing your work, be your own editor. Keep revising your work until you're certain that it's as good as it can be. That's your job. When that's done, it's time to start seeing if you're right.

14.11 Share Your Work

I merely leap and pause.

—Nijinsky

You cannot correct your work well until you've forgotten it.

—Voltaire

Waiting until you've forgotten your work to edit it is not a luxury that most writers have. Marty Asher, the senior division vice-president at Vintage Books, has a more modest idea: "Put your novel under your bed for thirty days." If you can't wait, at least give yourself a break from the book and share your manuscript with five kinds of readers who can advise you on how to improve it:

- Friends and family. They will tell you they like it because they like you. After all, what are friends and family for? You deserve encouragement, so enjoy it.

- Potential readers. They may not know good writing, but they know what they like. Would they buy your book if they found it in a bookstore?

- Literate, objective readers. They may not know about the kind of book you're writing, but they can tell you what's wrong with your manuscript as well as what's right with it.

- Experts who are knowledgeable about the subject of your book or the kind of novel you are writing. Ask authors in your professional network who have had similar books published to review your manuscript. If you are developing a controversial thesis, find a member of the opposition to go over it for you and try to poke holes in it. You may not gain a convert, but you might avoid embarrassing yourself later.

- The most valuable of all: a devil's advocate, a mentor who can and will combine truth and charity and spot every word, idea, character, punctuation mark, sentence, or incident that can be improved or removed. Devil's advocates are worth their weight in royalties.

If you're writing fiction, join or start a critique group, a tableful of writers who get together every week—in person or on-line—and discuss one another's work in progress.

Write this injunction in large letters on every copy of the proposal or manuscript that you share with your professional network: "Spare the reader, not the writer." Include a red pen. If you can't find anyone else, use your professional network or *Literary Market Place* to locate an experienced, reputable freelance editor to help you polish your manuscript.

14.12 Do a Final Revision

Because reactions, especially to fiction, are subjective, receiving more than one will prepare you for the varying responses your book will arouse. Follow only the advice that makes sense to you. As in all things, you must trust your instincts.

Once you've sorted out the opinions of others and feel ready to return to your manuscript with a fresh eye, do a final revision. Then it's time to see if you got it right.

Only one thing should be greater than your devotion to your craft: your devotion to your career. This is the subject of the most valuable chapter in this book.

15

Why Agents Prefer Pigs to Chickens

Making a 100 Percent Commitment to Your Career

In the making of ham and eggs, do you know what the difference is between the pig and the chicken? The chicken is involved, but the pig is committed.

> The world always steps aside for people who know where they're going.
>
> —*Miriam Viola Larsen, poet*

You are the most important factor in your success. A passionate devotion to writing your books and making them successful will make you irresistible to any agent or publisher. The following seven steps will show you how to make a 100 percent commitment to your career.

15.1 *Know Yourself and Your Goals*

> You can't have everything. Where would you put it?
> —*Ann Landers*

> Vision is the art of seeing things invisible.
> —*Jonathan Swift*

Life, like art, should be the celebration of a vision. Sue Grafton believes that "writing isn't something you do, it's something you are." To be a successful writer, you must know who you are and what you want. Tom Clancy once said, "Nothing is so real as a dream." However, the French poet Paul Valery believed this paradox: "The best way to make your dreams come true is to wake up." Take this opportunity to create a vision of yourself and your goals as a person and a writer.

Wolfgang Amadeus Mozart said, "When I am . . . completely myself, my ideas flow best and most abundantly." Well, on the literary chorus line of life, who are you, anyway? When a friend of Dorothy Parker had a baby, Parker sent her this cable: "Dear Mary: We all knew you had it in you." What have you got in you?

Make lists of your strengths and weaknesses as a person and a writer. What are the strengths you need to be a writer? A knowledge of books, writing, and what you're writing about, perhaps a desire to teach. Make lists of your personal and professional frailties and strong points.

Also make lists of the joys and hazards of writing. What are the hazards? (A book idea: the joys and hazards of different jobs to help people choose a career.) These lists must convince you that you have what it takes to make the grade. They must also justify your efforts. Keep these lists handy. Refer to them and revise them as needed.

Best-selling novelist Susan Isaacs once admitted that "hot fudge fills many needs." What needs does writing fill for you? Keeping in mind the need to harmonize the short view and the long view, make lists of your immediate and long-term personal goals. Does writing fit into them well?

The great German poet Johann Goethe believed that "life is the infancy of our immortality." (Does that make all books children's books?) Love, money, the need to communicate, and immortality inspire many writers to ply their craft.

When asked why he wrote the best-seller *The Name of the Rose*, Umberto Eco replied, "I felt like poisoning a monk." What are your literary goals? An aspiring writer once noted that every writer marches to a slightly different drummer.

In a William Hamilton cartoon, a young writer is musing wistfully to a companion: "Fame is such a hollow goal. Cult figure may be enough."

It's been said that goals are dreams with a deadline. What is the beat of your drummer? You can sum up your literary goals and your means to achieving them with the answers to the following nine questions. Start each answer with the word *I* and be specific. Answering these questions is an essential step in becoming a successful writer.

Your agent may ask you these questions, and you won't come across as a professional unless you have ready answers. The answers will also help clarify what you want your agent to accomplish for you.

1. Why do you want to write? You've already listed the joys of writing. What drives you to be a writer?

2. What literary forms—poetry, novels, nonfiction, plays, screenplays—do you want to write in? This is the easiest question.

3. What do you want your writing to communicate: knowledge, useful information, your philosophy, the variety and inexhaustible richness of people and life?

4. What do you want your writing to achieve? Herman Melville once wrote, "It is my earnest desire to write those sort of books which are said to 'fail.'" *Moby Dick* did fail when it was published in 1851, and Melville died forty years later without the recognition he deserved. Do you want your writing to provide pleasure, bring about social change, enable your readers to enjoy better lives?

5. Who are you writing for? An editor once told writer Arky Gonzales, "The subtle difference between a writer and an amateur is that amateurs feel and write for themselves; professional writers write for somebody else. This difference comes across in the very first or second line of an outline or manuscript." Are you writing to be read, or are you writing just for yourself? Your audience will determine what you write and how.

6. How much money a year do you want to earn from your writing? This question will yield the shortest answer of the nine. Establish financial as well as literary goals for your books. Figure out how much you want to earn from each book and what you want your annual income to be. Whether you want to earn a hundred or a million dollars a year, pick a round number. Your agent can give you a realistic perspective. For instance, if you want to earn $100,000 a year writing poetry, you'd better go back to the drawing board.

   Writers at our seminars say everything from nothing to millions. There are no wrong answers, but your answer has to correspond to what you produce. If you don't care how much money you earn a year from your writing, you can write anything.

   Mark Twain once admitted, "I'm opposed to millionaires, but it would be dangerous to offer me the position." If you want the position, there's only one kind of book you can write: best-sellers.

7. How involved do you want to get with the writing process? If you are a doctor who has a book's worth of information to communicate, don't feel that you have to become a writer to communicate that information. Your asset is your information, your credibility, and your ability to promote your book, not your ability to write it.

There's a *New Yorker* cartoon that shows a patient sitting in his doctor's examination room. The doctor says to him: "I'm afraid that novel in you will have to come out." There are more ways to get that book out of you than ever. You can

- Write it yourself

- Use a freelance editor or "book doctor" to help you

- Collaborate with another writer

- Hire a ghostwriter

As celebrity biographies prove, agents, editors, and book buyers don't care who writes a book, just as long as it delivers.

8. Do you want to self-publish, pay to be published, or be paid to be published? You have to decide how involved you want to get with the publishing process. You have more options than ever for getting your books published. You can self-publish them, which, thanks to the growth of desktop publishing and short-run printing, tens of thousands of writers are doing. You can pay part of the publishing costs to a subsidy publisher or all of the publishing costs to a vanity publisher.

You can have your book published by a small house, a large one, a regional publisher, a national one, a scholarly or university press, a publisher that does professional books, or a religious house.

9. How will you support your writing until it can support you? The average income of members of the Authors Guild is $7,500 a year. This helps to explain why a freelancer has been called a writer with a working spouse. After deciding what they want to write, the next question most writers have to answer is, How are you going to work to buy writing time?

Writer's Digest once ran a cartoon in which a wide-eyed woman sitting next to a man at a party says: "I'm so thrilled to meet an author. What do you do for a living?"

To help you weather the rough spots, take Sue Grafton's suggestion and create a five-year plan for your career. Decide where you would like to be five years from today, and then plan what you have to do, starting today, to reach that goal.

The answers to these questions should produce a coherent picture of your literary and financial goals. They should strike a realistic balance between writing for yourself and writing for the marketplace. They will make you sound more professional.

Put this list on the wall where you write. Make it your personal set of affirmations. Whenever you begin to wonder who you are or why you're writing, read the answers aloud to yourself. If the answers stop inspiring your best work, find new answers or another line of work.

15.2   Reinvent Yourself as an Infopreneur

A *New Yorker* cartoon shows a cornfield with two scarecrows standing in it. One is saying to the other, "English Lit. How about you?"

It's been said that if writers were good businesspeople, they'd have too much sense to be writers. It's important for you to think about business as well as writing. You are part of an entrepreneurial explosion that is one of the most hopeful signs for our future.

Despite the jokes about the hazards of being a literary entrepreneur that are scattered throughout this chapter, start thinking of yourself as an entrepreneur, a self-employed professional running a small business. Balance your desire to write something and the satisfaction of doing it well and seeing it published against your potential compensation and how the project will help develop your craft and your career, how it will help you reach your goals. Your agent will respect your professionalism.

Do you have well-designed business cards that say you're a writer? What about stationery? If you don't already have these things, get thee to a printer.

If you want to write fiction, you just have to keep at it until you're successful. If you write nonfiction, there are two contradictory approaches to developing your career, both of which have merit:

1. One editor suggests not getting fixed on a certain subject. There are many subjects and kinds of writing that can be developed to make a living. If editors are willing to pay you to learn about a subject that interests you, why not? Novelist Fenton Johnson recommends that writers diversify by writing fiction and nonfiction.

2. The second approach is a more effective way to build a career, which is why it's used by small publishers and booksellers. Practice "nichecraft." Develop a specialty. Once you've done one book on a subject, you're an authority and can present yourself as an expert when you try to sell your next book or article on the same subject.

After writing and self-publishing the first edition of *Earning Money Without a Job,* Jay Conrad Levinson has continued to write books about Guerrilla Marketing for entrepreneurs. At this writing, they number thirteen, and they create synergy by helping to sell one another as well as Levinson's audio- and videocassettes and his CD-ROM.

As a writer, your capital is your time, your ideas, and your ability to turn your ideas into salable material. Examine your ideas with an eye to recycling them in as many media as possible: articles in American and foreign trade and consumer magazines and newspapers that can be rewritten and resold, books, CD-ROMs, software, television shows, movies, audio- and videocassettes. Pick the right subject or kind of novel, and you can carve a career out of it.

After you've written one book, you can go from book to book and advance to advance. If you, your agent, or your editor has ideas and you put the proposals together, you can jump from one project into the next.

You have to keep generating ideas and proposals for nonfiction or whatever your editor needs to see for a novel. You can't assume that a publisher will buy all of them or that they will succeed if they are published. Danielle Steel once recalled that after her first novel was published, she wrote five more that have never been published.

The trade-off to practicing nichecraft, especially with fiction, is that once you become established as an author of a certain kind of book, you risk becoming typecast (pardon the pun). It may be harder to switch subjects or the kind of fiction you are writing. One way to get around this is to use a pseudonym. When Anne Rice takes a break from writing best-sellers about vampires, she uses two other names for her erotica.

Beyond thinking of yourself as an entrepreneur, think of yourself as an Infopreneur: an entrepreneur who makes a living coming up with ideas and communicating them in as many media and places as possible.

15.3 Mobilize Your Networks

When best-selling business-book author Harvey Mackay gives presentations, he asks, "What is the most important word in the English language?" His answer: Rolodex. Mackay's has 7,600 names in it.

Lily Tomlin once quipped, "Remember: We're all in this alone." Unless you collaborate, writing is a solitary endeavor, but being a writer doesn't have to be. The moment you were born, you had a personal network: your family. As you grew up, you enlarged your personal network with friends, schoolmates, and coworkers.

The following five suggestions will help you overcome the isolation of writing:

1. Develop two nationwide professional networks:

    - A publishing network with writers, editors, booksellers, reviewers, librarians, writing teachers, publicists, publishers' sales representatives, media people, reading groups, and fans of your work

    - A field network of every key person in politics, media, business, academia, and the government and professionals in the fields associated with what you're writing about, whether it's mysteries or health.

    Best-selling novelist Jacqueline Susann had a Christmas mailing list with 9,000 names on it. She took great pains to cultivate everyone in the business who could help her, and they did.

    You have both direct and indirect networks. Your direct network is all of the people you know; your indirect network is everyone they know. Continue to build your personal and professional networks throughout your career.

    Word of mouth is the best promotion. Your networks can be an effective national sales force helping you to generate "the big mo"— momentum for your book. They can be powerful allies in your quest for success.

2. Your computer modem can create an international network: You can communicate with people around the world on 60,000 bulletin boards covering just about every subject. In 1995, the number of people on-line was guesstimated to be 30 million and it was growing at the rate of 10 to 15 percent a month. The Internet, the network of networks, reaches 160 countries. In addition to the consolation and encouragement they can offer as friends, the on-line literary community is a valuable source of advice about agents, publishers, ideas, writing, research, and promotion.

3. Join local and national writers organizations and a critique group. Appendix 5 is a selected list of writers organizations. More are listed in *Literary Market Place* (LMP). You can also attend classes, seminars, conferences, and publishing institutes, which LMP also lists.

4. Keep up with the tomes. Stay abreast of the endless flow of books into which yours will merge. Browse in bookstores and ask booksellers about what's selling. To keep up with news about agents, writers and publishers, read *Coda, Writer's Digest, The Writer, Publishers Weekly,* and at least the Sunday book review section of the *New York Times,* and stay in touch with your professional network.

A book is a present you can open again and again.
—Sign in a San Francisco bookstore

---

5. Support the business you want to support you. Three of the joys of the literary life are browsing in bookstores, buying books, and building a library of books you love. Whether you buy hardcovers or paperbacks, whether you're buying them as gifts or for yourself, buy books. Book lovers never go to bed alone.

Try working in a bookstore or being an unpaid intern. Get to know your local booksellers, and make allies of them. They may share your love of books and can be valuable sources of information and encouragement. They may be able to help you find an agent. One day, you will be asking them for a book signing!

Encourage people you know to read, and exchange books with them. This is a slow but certain way to build an audience for your work.

15.4   Do Everything You Can for Your Books

Just as your agent is your advocate, you have to be the advocate for your book. You can do a dozen things to help make the birth of your baby a celebration:

1. If editors are interested in acquiring your book, visit them if you can. Editors will have varying degrees of passion for a book, and houses will have different levels of commitment to it, depending on their response to your book and their success with similar books. Meeting editors and their colleagues will give you a good idea of how happy your working marriage will be. The more impressed they are with you and your future, the better the offer they'll make.

2. Make sure that the nonfiction manuscript you write fulfills or exceeds the promise of your proposal, or that you have revised your novel according to your editor's suggestions. Get feedback on the manuscript from readers. Make the manuscript impeccable in form and content. The harder editors have to work editing a manuscript, the more discouraged they may become about its potential.

3. Ask for a time line on the publication of your book and monitor its progress as it makes its way through production. Use *The Writer's Workbook: A Full and Friendly Guide to Boosting Your Book's Sales,* by Judith Applebaum and Florence Janovic, as a guide.

4. If you have an idea for a jacket or cover, send the editor a note about it, do a rough sketch, or if you have access to an artist, have a design done. Even if it's not used, but it may help the cover designer.

5. Write the jacket or cover copy for your book. It may not be used, but it will give your publisher something to improve on.

6. Ask for samples of your publisher's publicity materials, and write your own.

7. Visit your publisher after your book has been accepted but before the marketing plans are set. Meet all of the staff members involved with the editing, production, and marketing of your book, and discuss their marketing plan. Learn from them how you can help make your book sell. Express your gratitude for their help.

8. Take your local sales rep to lunch and absorb all you can about the business. Find out how you can help.

9. Visit local booksellers and get them excited enough about your book so that they and their staffs will "handsell" it.

10. Ask your editor to help you monitor sales through bookstores, local distributors, and national wholesalers.

11. Buy a lifetime supply of your books. If your publisher sells out and decides not to go back to press, you will not have the chance to buy a stash of them for future use.

12. Part of the challenge is being an advocate for your book without becoming obnoxious. Don't badger anyone with phone calls. Create a paper trail with notes instead.

In the course of following these suggestions, you will discover other opportunities. After writing your book as well as you can, promoting it is the most important way that you can help your book succeed.

15.5 Promote Your Books

> Marketing has become almost synonymous with publishing.
> *−The New York Times*, 1996

> Two cannibals are having dinner and one says to the other: "You know, I don't like your publisher."
> "OK," the other cannibal replies, "then just eat the noodles."

> Marketing has long been the industry's weakest link.
> *−John Dessauer*, Book Publishing: The Basic Introduction

The most common reason authors become disenchanted with their publishers is the lack of promotion. Unless a book is one of the few big titles on a list, an author will usually be dissatisfied with what the publisher is doing to promote the book.

In *The Writer's Quotation Book: A Literary Companion*, editor Jim Charlton quotes humorist Robert Benchley: "It took me fifteen years to discover I had no talent for writing, but I couldn't give it up because by that time, I was too famous." If fame is your goal, and you don't want to wait fifteen years for it, give yourself a promotion. Sandy Dijkstra believes that making a book successful requires overcoming three levels of indifference: in agents, publishers, and book buyers.

A recreational pilot once observed, "In flying an airplane, the hardest thing you have to deal with is the ground." The hardest thing in writing is getting a book off it. Writing a book, getting an agent, and selling a book to a publisher are easy compared to making the book successful.

It's been said that 80 percent of a major publisher's promotion budget goes to 20 percent of its books. That leaves 20 percent of the budget for the other 80 percent of the list.

There are two polar opposite views you can take about promotion. One is suggested by Knopf marketing director Carl Lennertz, who once affirmed, "I truly believe that a wonderful book will succeed with no marketing whatsoever." You can do nothing and hope that lightning strikes. If you understand that every book is a stepping-stone to the next one, you can take the opposite tack and assume that if you don't promote your book, it won't get done and the book will fail, making the next book harder to sell.

There are more ways to promote your books than ever, and a promotable author is the best selling tool a publisher has (pun intended). As Vintage Books executive Marty Asher has said: "The best promotion department for your book is you." However, many authors can't promote their books; others won't. Without a news angle or a famous or promotable personality behind it, a novel is tougher to publicize than nonfiction.

If you are published by a large house and your book is not receiving top-of-the-line treatment, it will be one of many. Assume that no one knows or cares as much about your book as you do, and that only your editor has read it. Assume that communications between the advertising, editorial, publicity, and sales departments are not perfect. All this means is that if you want the public to find out about your book, you either have to let fate take its course or work damn hard to promote it.

Publishers have a short- and long-term perspective on promotion. They're eager to find writers whose livelihoods depend on their going around the country giving seminars and selling books. That's a lifetime promotion plan for every book they write.

Most books have a six-week window of opportunity to sink or swim in the ceaseless waves of new books, bobbing along on promotion that generates sales. That window opens on the publication date when, theoretically at least, books are in stores and reviews start to appear.

One sure way to impress an agent is with your plans for promoting your book. Jack Canfield and Mark Victor Hansen spent a year promoting *Chicken Soup for the Soul,* before it hit the best-seller list. Canfield advises writers to "spend 90 percent of your time selling, marketing and self-promoting your book."

A *Writer's Digest* cartoon shows a guy sitting at a bar, lamenting to a fellow tippler, "Since I started freelancing full-time, I've made quite a few sales . . . my house, my car, my furniture . . ."

Take the long view about promotion. Look at it as a lifelong challenge at which you will become more effective with each book. When reporters and talk-show hosts invite you back and your promotional efforts boost the sales of your book, you will find the process exciting.

Trying to convince millions of book buyers across the country to buy your book will probably be the hardest thing you have ever done, much harder than writing your book. Set realistic goals for what to expect of your book and yourself.

Don't get involved with promotion halfheartedly. You've got to convince yourself and your publisher that you harbor a consuming lust for success and that you are irresistibly driven to do whatever it takes to make your books sell. Unless you jump into promotion body and soul, you may be better off working on your next book.

Let your agent help you be realistic about balancing your efforts against the sales they may produce, the enjoyment you get out of promotion, and the need to use your time as productively as possible. Depending on your goals, your personality, the kind of books you write, and your need to earn a living, you might be right to decide that you, your publisher, and your readers will be better served if you keep your cheeks glued to a chair and your fingertips on a keyboard.

When you submit your proposal or manuscript, describe your speaking, media, and promotional experience. Present a plan listing what you will do to promote your book. Your eagerness and ability to promote your work will be a major factor in determining the editor, publisher, and deal you get for your book. Appendix 4 includes promotion ideas, but for a comprehensive guide to promotion, read John Kremer's *1,001 Ways to Promote Your Book*.

A poet laments to a friend: "Burglars broke into my house last night."
Friend: "Yes? What happened?"
The poet: "They searched through every room, then left a $5 bill on my dresser."

—10,000 Jokes, Toasts, and Stories

15.6   Keep Growing

Don't allow your drive to be a successful writer turn you into a one-sided personality. Strive to develop all of your potentials as a human being. Your writing will mirror your personal growth.

In his excellent book, *This Business of Writing*, Gregg Levoy writes, "The depth of your writing is a function of how absorbent you are. Writers must first inhale the world, and then exhale it in writing. Art, it has been said, is the discharge of experience, and the more deeply informed you are by your receptivity, by your life's experiences, the richer your writing. Imagine your body as a prism which the light of experience flows through and emerges as art. The more of the world you 'in-spire' (literally 'breathe in'), the more you are capable of inspiring the world."

15.7   Don't Let Anything—Especially Fear, Fame, or Fortune—Stop You

> The surest way to kill an artist is to give him everything he wants.
> –Henry Miller

The most remarkable story of perseverance I know is that of Jack Canfield and Mark Victor Hansen. After their agent, AAR member and author of the *Insider's Guide* Jeff Herman, received thirty-three rejections, he gave up. Armed with backpacks and manuscripts, Canfield and Hansen went to the American Booksellers Association convention. Four hundred publishers refused to look at the manuscript. Finally, Health Communications paid a small advance for *Chicken Soup for the Soul*, and the rest is publishing history.

It's been estimated that less than 1 percent of the practitioners of any art make a living at it. Yet writing is the easiest of the arts to enter: You just sit down and start writing. It's easier to succeed as an author than as an artist, actor, dancer, musician, or composer.

However, like agents and editors, you must develop a tolerance for uncertainty, disappointment, and rejection. Rejection comes with the territory. The *New Yorker* rejected a short story by Saul Bellow *after* he won the Nobel Prize. While your agent is trying to place your book, even if it doesn't sell, keep writing and take the long view.

Look at a rejection as the agent's or editor's loss. Agents and editors aren't judging you, they're judging your work, and if you've done everything you can to make your book as good as it can be, assume that they're wrong. Don't regard unsold work as a failure; regard it as inventory that one day will sell.

Even if your book does sell, once you type the last period on your manuscript, it's either terminal or timeless, and there's nothing you can do about it. Look at the fruits of your career not as one book but as ten or twenty, and make each better than the last.

Ray Bradbury once remarked, "When you start writing, you have to learn to accept rejection. Once you're successful, you have to learn to reject acceptance." Like publishers, writers can become prisoners of their success. You may disagree, but I think obscurity is one of a writer's greatest assets. Cherish your obscurity while you still have it. Use it to write, free from the distractions of fame and fortune and the pressure of expectations created by success.

Hundreds of agents and editors across the country are hungry for new writers. If you have enough talent and persistence, an agent and an editor, properly presented with the right manuscript at the right time, will take on your book.

Suzanne Lipsett, a freelance editor, novelist, and author of *Surviving a Writer's Life*, defined her approach to her writing like this: "Whatever I have to do to keep my family alive and my art alive, that's what I do." Here's a quick test of your commitment to your career. The highest score is nothing. Make a list of everything that is *more* important to you than becoming a successful author. The shorter the list, the more likely you'll make it.

There's a *New Yorker* cartoon showing a man and a woman sitting on a couch talking. The man is saying, "Look, I'm not talking about a lifetime commitment. I'm talking about marriage." Ultimately, this book isn't about agenting, writing, or publishing; it's about commitment. I can guarantee that the advice in this book works. Only you can guarantee that you will make the commitment to use it.

Failure is the path of least persistence. Because rejecting best-sellers is a publishing tradition, no matter how many times your work is rejected, you must keep writing and console yourself with the certainty that persistence rewards talent. A diamond is a piece of coal that stuck to the job.

A respected editor used to offer the following advice to aspiring writers: "If anything can stop you from becoming a writer, let it. If nothing can stop you, do it and you'll make it." I hope that you will let nothing stop you, that no matter what you write, you will commit yourself to becoming the best writer you can be, not just for yourself, but for all of us.

Writing High

The End of the Beginning

The greatest opportunity in business today is having a clean sheet of paper.

> —*Michael Treacy, coauthor of* The Discipline of Market Leaders

A good book is the purest essence of the human soul.

> —*Thomas Carlyle*

16.1 Why Now Is the Best Time to Be a Writer

There is a revolution going on and nobody knows where it's headed. I think I have a clearer vision than most, and that vision is big. There are no limitations.

> —*Tom Clancy*

If you are writing to meet the needs of the marketplace, and you have the ability to promote your work, now is the best time ever to be a writer. There are more

- Subjects to write about
- Books available
- Models for you to emulate
- Formats in which your books can be published
- Media for communicating your ideas

- Countries in which your books can be sold

- Agents

- Publishers

- Writers groups, classes, conferences, organizations, publishing institutes, magazines, and newsletters

- Ways to get your books written

- Options for getting your books published

- Bright, dedicated editors

- Good books being published

- Ways to promote your books

- Ways to make money from your ideas

than ever.

More Americans are reading books than ever, and it's possible to sell more copies of a book than ever. In addition, there is more money to be made from your ideas than ever. So if one's primary interest is money, it's the best time ever to be an agent as well as a writer. There are also more ways to make a living as a writer than ever.

16.2   Why Now Is the Most Exciting Time to Be Alive

We are as gods and might as well get good at it.
     —*Stewart Brand,* The Whole Earth Catalog *(1968)*

Information is coin of the realm in cyberspace.
     —*Charles Rubin, coauthor of* Guerrilla Marketing Online: The
          Entrepreneur's Guide to Earning Profits
               on the Internet

Thomas Jefferson thought that a revolution every so often can be a good thing. Technophiles believe that the three great events in human history are the inventions of writing, machinery, and the computer. For them, computer technology has sparked the greatest revolution in communication since Johannes Gutenberg invented the printing press 500 years ago.

Now is the most exciting time ever to be alive. Civilization is either at the beginning of the end or the end of the beginning. It's reinventing itself before our eyes. Life itself is miraculous, but we are living in the age of miracles. The continual breakthroughs in technology and genetic engineering are astonishing. It will one day be possible to store all sixteen million volumes in the Library of Congress on a disk the size of a penny. We are living on what has been called "the vertical slope of technology," and technology will not allow the rate of progress to slow down.

Microcomputer efficiency is doubling every eighteen months. Computers are transforming the way books are written, edited, designed, manufactured, sold, promoted, and used. They are also enlarging the markets both for books about the new technology and for electronic media, such as software, data bases, CD-ROMs, and on-line services.

There's a *New Yorker* cartoon that shows two dogs sitting in front of a computer and one is saying to the other, "On the Internet, nobody knows I'm a dog." Computers have cut the drudgery of writing while exploding the possibilities for research, networking, creativity, collaboration, and enterprise. Nicholas Negroponte, the author of the best-seller *Being Digital*, predicts that by 2000, a billion people will be on-line.

16.3 Why Content Is King

It is only with the heart that one can see rightly; what is essential · is invisible to the eye.

–*Antoine de Saint-Exupéry*, The Little Prince

Inner space is the real frontier.

–*Gloria Steinem*

Despite the miracles that are transforming our lives, people's needs haven't changed: physical and financial security; physical and mental health and peace of mind; a network of friends, family, and colleagues; meaningful work; sexual satisfaction; the opportunity to develop all of one's potential; an environment conducive to fulfilling one's needs; and hope for the future. After basic needs are met, the most important things in life remain invisible: love, faith, virtue, beauty, creativity, friendship, peace of mind, a sense of achievement, and a spirit of community.

What does all of this mean to you, as a writer? It's been said that luck is ability meeting opportunity. If this is true, then you are part of the luckiest generation of writers that ever lived.

Information is also doubling every eighteen months. You absorb more information in a month than people in the nineteenth century received in their whole lives. Information workers make up half of the American work force. The age of information, which is just beginning, has to be the age of the writer.

In one of Bruce Springsteen's songs, he complains about fifty-seven channels with nothing on. Before long, you will have 500 channels to choose from. You can promote, sell, and publish your books on-line. Author Steven Levy predicts that as television and computers merge, the World Wide Web will unleash 500 million channels. That's why content is king. Somebody has to fill the pipes.

Bookstores already have books on all of the needs mentioned at the beginning of this section. They contain endless possibilities for fiction and nonfiction. More continue to be published because what you need and care about are the same things that everyone else in the human family needs and cares about. This includes the inevitable problems that technology creates. You can tell that the Internet is starting to come of age when there is a 12-step program for overcoming addiction to it!

Change is the sacrifice required for progress. Whether you're writing fiction or nonfiction, you can help us all understand what to do, how to do it, and what it means. You can put information in the service of transformation.

16.4 Books and the Other Four Bs

Writing . . . is the great invention of the world.

–*Abraham Lincoln*

In the 1890s, people thought that books were in jeopardy because bicycles were so popular. In 1900, an article in a Saint Louis newspaper expressed concern for the future of books because people were spending so much time riding the new streetcars. Around this time, Congress considered a bill abolishing the patent office because some members felt that nothing more could be invented. The bill failed, but the inventions that followed continued to alarm book lovers.

According to the doomsday prophets, the radio, movies, television, and the computer were all supposed to sound the death knell for books. Books survived and are reused more than any of the other media. Can you imagine an officer of the court holding out a CD-ROM of the Bible for witnesses to take an oath?

It's been said that for a medium of communication to become integrated into our lives, it has to be usable in the four B's: bed, bath, beach, and bus. You can order and receive books on your computer, but I can't imagine the day when readers would want to curl up with a flat screen to read *War and Peace*.

Rather than being a threat to books, technology will liberate the medium to do what it does best. Nothing else offers the tactile feeling and experience of reading a book. As an affordable, efficient, portable, durable, sometimes beautiful, sometimes sacred means of communication, books will remain part of our lives. Despite the growing interest in electronic media, Simon & Schuster president Jon Newcomb spoke for most publishers when he vowed that at S & S, "Books will always be our cornerstone."

16.5 *Graduation Day*

Bob Hope was once talking at a college graduation when he was asked to give the graduates some advice about going out into the real world. His advice was "Don't go." If you are determined to go out into the real world of publishing and you want to be a successful author, there are six challenges for you to meet. You have to

- Write every day

- Take the long view as well as the short view in developing your books, your craft, and your career

- Set literary and financial goals for yourself that motivate you to produce your best work

- Keep writing books that you are proud of and that you can promote and recycle in as many media and countries as possible

- Never submit anything until it's 100 percent—as well conceived and well crafted as you can make it

- Always be 100 percent committed to achieving your goals

You know more and care more about your books and your career than anyone else, so you must be 100 percent committed to your success.

Chapter 13 describes a book's seven lunges at the brass ring of best-sellerdom. One more lunge is essential. It's the first lunge and the one you make by yourself. The strongest hope your books will have of reaching their literary and commercial potential is for you to stretch your abilities to their limits. Conceive and craft your books as well as only you can.

Submitting only your best work will bring out the best in every editor and agent who reads it.

16.6 Writing As If Books Mattered

Artists are the antennae of the race.

−Ezra Pound

Art is not a mirror held up to reality, but a hammer with which to shape it.

−Bertolt Brecht

Technology, the media, universal concerns, and the global culture and economy are uniting the human family for the first time. As the planet hurtles through time and space on this voyage of accelerating transformation into an unknowable future, Spaceship Earth has no more valuable passengers than its artists and writers, who should be its copilots.

The ancient Greek philosopher Heracleitus believed that "only change endures." The world is changing faster than ever, and readers of all ages around the world need reporters and storytellers to explain what's going on and how to survive and thrive as the age of information transforms our lives. Ideas can travel and transform readers just as they are transformed by the media used to communicate them.

Rarely has there been a greater need for calming, reassuring, inspiring words that help us understand ourselves and the world around us. We need your voice, your vision, your passion, and your humor as much as they were ever needed.

Former New York mayor and best-selling author Ed Koch once said, "Books are not the foundation of civilization, they *are* civilization." Max Perkins was a legendary editor who worked for Scribner's. In a career that spanned three decades, he edited the work of Ernest Hemingway, F. Scott Fitzgerald, and Thomas Wolfe. In *Max Perkins: Editor of Genius*, Scott Berg's inspiring biography, Perkins says, "There is nothing so important as the book can be." The right book, fiction or nonfiction, will change the world. Norman Mailer believes that "only great fiction can save the world . . . for fiction still believes that one mind can see it whole."

Even if you are not fated to write books that improve the human condition, writing any book well is an achievement of which you can be proud. Writing is a courageous calling, and if you can add to the world's store of pleasure and information, of beauty and truth, your future is assured.

If your books are touched with magic because of their ideas or their style, if you capture people, places, and situations in a compelling, timeless, universal way, your books will find their audience no matter how they are published, and they will endure. What greater challenge could you ask for? What greater achievement could you hope for?

Author Barry Lopez once remarked that "sometimes a person needs a story more than food to stay alive." People everywhere are hungry for information and understanding, and the more they know, the more they want to know.

16.7 A Fork in the Road

Writers ask agents, "What do editors really want?" What editors really want is writers like these:

- Humorist James Thurber, who said: "If I couldn't write, I couldn't live."

- The woman at a writers conference who admitted, "My husband just ran off with the baby-sitter, and I'm trying to figure how to use it in my novel."

- Isaac Bashevis Singer, the Nobel Prize–winning author whose mother asked at his birth, "Is it a boy or a girl?" "Neither one," replied the midwife. "It's a writer."

- Isaac Asimov, who wrote and edited 470 books and anthologies without an agent and once said: "If the doctor told me I only had six minutes to live, I'd type a little faster."

Editors and agents are looking for writers who love to write, who *live* to write. As San Francisco Bay Area agent Felicia Eth said, they're looking for "writers who make them forget that they're in the business and make them remember *why* they're in the business."

Always remember that as a writer, you are the most important person in the publishing process because you make it go. The more competitive the book business gets, the more agents' and editors' jobs hinge on their ferreting out good books and new writers. Promising new writers are the lifeblood of the publishing and agenting business. Agents and editors are as delighted to find promising new writers as new writers are to be published. Selling a well-conceived, well-written book that satisfies the growing, insatiable need for understanding and entertainment of readers around the world is easier than ever.

Baseball great Yogi Berra once said, "When you come to a fork in the road, take it." I hope that this book will be a fork in the road for you. Whether it inspires you to hit the keys or take up cooking, it will have served you well.

The Chinese sage Lao-tzu taught that "he who obtains has little. He who scatters has much." The simplest recipe for happiness that I know of is to find your unique gift and give it to the world.

If you are lucky enough to be able to write, you have been endowed with a wonderful gift. You owe it to yourself and posterity to develop your gift to its fullest, to place your life in the service of your gift, your ideas, and your readers.

I can promise you that the right combination of talent, luck, and perseverance will lead to success. The only absolute about writing, agenting, and publishing is to trust your instincts and common sense and do whatever works. Good luck!

Appendixes

Appendix 1

Sample Agent's Clauses

The following two agent's clauses, the second one ours, are used in publishers' contracts. Agents who don't have written agreements with their clients may, as in the first example, spell out their compensation in the agent's clause of the publisher's contract more completely than would otherwise be necessary.

First Agent's Clause

The Author hereby irrevocably appoints_____
_____ as his sole and exclusive agent with respect to the said Work and authorizes and directs the Publisher to make all payments due or to become due to the Author hereunder to and in the name of the said agent, and to accept the receipt of the said agent as full evidence and satisfaction of such payments. As sole and exclusive agent, the said agent is authorized to negotiate for the Author throughout the World as to the disposal of all other rights in and to the said Work. The said agent is further empowered to engage sub-agents for the sale of British Commonwealth and/or translation rights in and to the said Work and to pay such sub-agents a commission of up to ten percent (10%) of the monies collected from the disposition of any such British Commonwealth and/or translation rights through such sub-agents. In consideration for services rendered, the said agent is entitled to receive or retain as its commission fifteen percent (15%) of gross monies paid to the Author hereunder and from all other rights in and to the said Work (including the said optioned works), except that such commission shall be reduced to ten percent (10%) as to those monies out of which a sub-agent's commission of five percent (5%) or more is

also paid, the said ten percent (10%) to be computed after deduction of the sub-agent's commissions. The provisions of this clause shall survive the expiration of this Agreement.

Second Agent's Clause

The Author irrevocably assigns to Michael Larsen/Elizabeth Pomada Literary Agents, 1029 Jones Street, San Francisco, CA 94109 ("the Agent"), 15% of all monies due to the author under this Agreement. The Author authorizes the Agent to receive all monies payable to the Author through this Agreement. The Agent is authorized to act on the Author's behalf in all matters arising out of this Agreement. This clause will survive the termination of this Agreement.

Appendix 2

Sample Author-Agent Contracts

The following three sample author-agent contracts will give you a sense of the range that these agreements can take.

First Sample Contract

It is agreed that _____ (hereinafter referred to as the Client) does grant _____ (hereinafter referred to as the Agent) the exclusive right to represent the Client in any and all negotiations for the sale of _____ (hereinafter referred to as the Work) to a publisher and, thereafter, for the sale of any and all rights related to the Work as well as all other books and/or projects as shall be mutually agreed upon.

The Client does hereby warrant that He is the author and sole owner of the Work; that it is original and that it contains no matter unlawful in the content nor does it violate the rights of any third party; that the rights granted hereunder are free and clear; and that the Client has full power to grant such representation to the Agent.

The Client agrees that the Agent shall receive 15% (fifteen percent) of the gross of all monies earned from the sale of the Work. It is also agreed that the Agent will receive from the sale, licensing option or other disposition of any foreign language rights (including British rights) when negotiated without an overseas sub-agent a commission of 15% (fifteen percent) of the gross; when foreign language volume rights (including British rights) are negotiated with an overseas sub-agent the total commission will be 20% (twenty percent) of the gross: 10% (ten percent) for the Agent and 10% (ten percent) for the sub-agent. Further, if the Agent should use the services of a sub-agent for the sale of movie and/or television rights the total commission shall be 20% (twenty percent): 10% (ten percent) for the agent and 10% (ten percent) for the sub-agent . . . all from the gross.

The Client does hereby empower the Agent to receive all monies due to him under any contractual arrangements related to the Work and the Agent warrants that her receipt shall be a good and valid discharge. The Client further empowers the Agent to deal with all parties on his behalf in all matters arising from the Work. The Client agrees that this agreement shall be binding on his estate.

The Agent agrees to remit all monies due to the Client, less the Agent's stipulated commission, within thirty (30) days of the receipt of any monies earned from the sale of any rights related to the Work if said monies are paid in U.S. currency. Otherwise, the Agent will remit all monies due to the Client, less the Agent's stipulated commission, within thirty (30) days of the conversion of said monies to U.S. currency.

If either Client or Agent should desire to terminate this agreement either party must inform the other, by certified mail, of such intent, and the agreement shall be considered terminated 60 (sixty) days after receipt of such letter. It is, however, understood that any monies due after termination whether derived from contractual agreements already negotiated or under negotiation by the Agent when the agreement is terminated shall be paid to the Agent who will then deduct her commission and remit to the Client as outlined above.

If the foregoing correctly sets forth your understanding please sign both copies of this letter where indicated, retaining one copy for your files and returning the other copy to me for mine.

Second Sample Contract

Another agent drew up the following agreement with the help of a literary lawyer. This agent uses an American foreign rights representative who charges 20 percent to help sell foreign rights, so the commission rises to 30 percent.

Dear writer:

On the following terms, I hereby propose to act as your agent to seek publication of your book and works derived from it, tentatively titled _____ and referred to below as the "Property."

1.   EXCLUSIVE AGENT I will be your exclusive agent for the Property and any sequels to it (works on the same subject as the Property,

making use of the same themes and written for the same market) for an indefinite period beginning today, [date]. However, I will be entitled to commissions beyond termination according to paragraph 5 below.

2. TERMINATION This agreement can and will be terminated by either party upon mailing a written 90-day notice to terminate to the other party. However, I will be entitled to commissions beyond termination according to paragraph 5 below.

3. REASONABLE EFFORTS I will make every reasonable effort to obtain the best possible offer for the Property. I will report to you immediately any offer that I obtain, and will generally keep you informed of my activities under this contract.

4. AUTHORITY Any offer that I may succeed in obtaining will be subject to your written acceptance, and will have no binding effect on you otherwise. You will be free to accept or reject any offer. My authority will be limited to obtaining offers. I will have no power or authority to close any sale or to make any binding commitment of any kind on your behalf.

5. COMMISSIONS If during the period of this agreement I bring you an offer that you accept in writing, and you and the publisher execute the publishing agreement, you will pay me a commission equal to fifteen percent of all proceeds received from the publisher. In addition, you will pay me a commission equal to thirty percent from sales throughout the rest of the world and from the sale of any serial, merchandising, or dramatic (motion picture, television, radio) rights when a sub-agent is required to negotiate the deal. In addition, I will receive the same percentages (15% when a sub-agent is not used and 30% when a sub-agent is used) of all proceeds obtained from any subsequent sale of rights that derives from the initial sale of the Property, including, but not limited to the following: condensation, translation, anthology, periodicals, electronic formats and reproductions, television, audio and video recordings, paperback, and commercial. If you sell or transfer publishing rights in the Property to a person or company to which I submitted a proposal for the sale of those rights during the term of this agreement, I will be entitled to my full commission even though the sale or transfer of rights takes place after the agreement terminates. My right to compensation for a sale or disposition of rights under this agreement, once earned, will continue even after the agreement terminates, and in case of my death or disability, my successor in interest will have that right and will administer the receipt and disbursement of funds under this agreement.

6.   PROCEEDS I will be entitled to collect on your behalf all proceeds derived from the sale of the Property. I will deduct my commissions and forward all sums due to you along with any statements from the publisher or licensee within three weeks of my receipt of proceeds or statements from the publisher or licensee.

7.   COSTS You will repay me for all postage, copying, telephone, travel, and other costs specifically related to the sale of the Property. These costs will not exceed $300 without your consent. I will be entitled to deduct these costs, as well as my commission, from the proceeds derived from the sale of the property if you have not reimbursed me already.

8.   COMPETING WORKS As a literary agent, I may represent clients whose work competes with yours. You agree that I may do so.

9.   ARBITRATION We will arbitrate any dispute arising under this agreement before an arbitrator in San Francisco, California, under the rules for commercial disputes of the American Arbitration Association then in effect. If we cannot agree on the arbitrator, each of us will appoint one representative, and the representatives will choose the arbitrator. The arbitration award will be enforceable in any court with jurisdiction.

10.   ATTORNEY'S FEES If any dispute is referred to arbitration or results in litigation, the party who wins shall be entitled to reasonable attorney's fees from the other party.

11.   ASSIGNMENT Neither party will assign or pledge his or her rights under this agreement without written consent of the other party.

12.   INDEMNIFICATION You represent and warrant to me that you have the right to make this agreement without impairing anyone else's rights, and you agree not to make any commitment about the Property or works derived from it that conflicts with this agreement. You will indemnify me and hold me harmless against any claim based on your breach of the provisions of this paragraph.

13.   ENTIRE AGREEMENT This agreement supersedes any and all other agreements between us with respect to the Property and is the only agreement between us on its subject. It may be amended only in writing signed by both of us.

If the above terms are acceptable to you, please indicate by signing below and returning this agreement to me. It will then constitute a binding agreement between us.

Third Sample Contract

Michael Larsen/Elizabeth Pomada Literary Agents

Dear Michael and Elizabeth:

While trust, friendliness, and confidence are the basis for our relationship, I have read your brochure, and I am ready to put our commitments to each other in writing:

I appoint you my sole agent to advise me and negotiate sales of all kinds for all of my literary material and its subsidiary rights in all forms and media and for all future uses throughout the world. You may appoint coagents to help you. If you say that you can't handle a property, I shall be free to do as I please with it without obligation to you.

If a potential buyer for my literary work or writing services approaches me, I will refer the buyer to you.

If an idea is mine and we do not develop it together, only I have the rights to the idea or any basic variation on it. However, if another writer approaches you with the same idea or a similar idea, you are free to represent the project.

If the idea for a project is yours, only you have the rights to the idea or any basic variation on it. You may represent a project competitive to mine, provided that we agree that it doesn't lessen your ability to represent my work.

You will pay for all expenses which arise in selling my work except photocopying my work; mailing it abroad or on multiple submissions; buying galleys and books; and legal assistance. I must approve all expenses of more than $50 for which I will be responsible.

You may receive on my behalf all money due me from agreements signed through your efforts. This includes all sales for which negotiations begin during the term of this agreement, and all changes and extensions in those agreements, regardless of when they are made or by whom.

You are irrevocably entitled to deduct 15% commission on all gross income earned through your agency for my writing services. For foreign rights, you may deduct 20%, which includes 10% for your coagents. All commissions you receive will not be returnable for any reason.

I must approve all offers and sign all agreements negotiated on my behalf. Michael Larsen/Elizabeth Pomada Literary Agents will be named as my agency in all agreements I sign on all projects that you represent.

You will remit all money and statements due me within 10 working days of receiving them.

You may respond to mail received on my behalf unless it is personal, in which case you will forward it to me promptly. I will notify you promptly if I change my phone number or address.

I realize that it may take years to sell a book, and you agree to try as long as you believe it is possible. You will notify me promptly when you can no longer help on a book. Then I may do as I wish with it without obligation to you.

If a problem arises about your efforts or our relationship, I will contact you, and we will conscientiously try to solve the problem with fairness to both of us. A problem we can't solve will be resolved with a mediator or arbitrator we choose.

You or I may end this agreement with 60 days' notice by registered mail. However, you will be entitled to receive statements and commissions on all rights on properties on which you make the initial sale, whether or not the agency represents me on the sales of these rights.

This agreement is binding on our respective personal and business heirs and assigns, and will be interpreted according to California law.

I am free to sign this agreement and will not agree to a conflicting obligation. I will sign two copies, and each of us will have one. Both of our signatures are needed to change this agreement.

We sign this agreement with the hope that it will symbolize our mutual long-term commitment to the development of my career and to sharing the rewards of this growth.

Appendix 3

The Code of Ethics for the Association of Authors' Representatives (AAR)

The following is the code of ethics that all AAR members must agree, in writing, to uphold.

Association of Authors' Representatives, Inc.
Canon of Ethics

1.   The members of the Association of Authors' Representatives, Inc. are committed to the highest standard of conduct in the performance of their professional activities. While affirming the necessity and desirability of maintaining their full individuality and freedom of action, the members pledge themselves to loyal service to their clients' business and artistic needs, and will allow no conflicts of interest that would interfere with such service. They pledge their support to the Association itself and to the principles of honorable coexistence, directness, and honesty in their relationships with their co-members. They undertake never to mislead, deceive, dupe, defraud, or victimize their clients, other members of the Association, the general public, or any other person with whom they do business as a member of the Association.

2.   Members shall take responsible measures to protect the security and integrity of clients' funds. Members must maintain separate bank accounts for money due their clients so that there is no commingling of clients' and members' funds. Members shall deposit funds received on behalf of clients promptly upon receipt, and shall make payments of domestic earnings due clients promptly, but in no event later than ten business days after clearance. Revenues from foreign rights over $50

shall be paid to clients within ten business days after clearance. Sums under $50 shall be paid within a reasonable time of clearance. However, on stock and similar rights, statements of royalties and payments shall be made not later than the month following the member's receipt, each statement and payment to cover all royalties received to the 25th day of the previous calendar month. Payments for amateur rights shall be made not less frequently than every six months. A member's books of account must be open to the client at all times with respect to transactions concerning the client.

3.   In addition to the compensation for agency services that is agreed upon between a member and a client, a member may, subject to the approval of the client, pass along charges incurred by the member on the client's behalf, such as copyright fees, manuscript retyping, photocopies, copies of books for use in the sale of other rights, long distance calls, special messenger fees, etc. Such charges shall only be made if the client has agreed to reimburse such expenses.

4.   A member shall keep each client apprised of matters entrusted to the member and shall promptly furnish such information as the client may reasonably request.

5.   Members shall not represent both buyer and seller in the same transaction. Except as provided in the next sentence, a member who represents a client in the grant of rights in any property owned or controlled by the client may not accept any compensation or other payment from the acquirer of such rights, including but not limited to so-called "packaging fees," it being understood that the member's compensation, if any, shall be derived solely from the client. Notwithstanding the foregoing, a member may accept (or participate in) a so-called "packaging fee" paid by an acquirer of television rights to a property owned or controlled by a client if the member: a) fully discloses to the client at the earliest practical time the possibility that the member may be offered such a "packaging fee" which the member may choose to accept; b) delivers to the clients at such time a copy of the Association's statement regarding packaging and packaging fees; and c) offers the client at such time the opportunity to arrange for other representation in the transaction. In no event shall the member accept (or participate in) both a packaging fee and compensation from the client with respect to the transaction. For transactions subject to Writers Guild of America (WGA) jurisdiction, the regulations of the WGA shall take precedence over the requirements of this paragraph.

6. Members may not receive a secret profit in connection with any transaction involving a client. If such a profit is received, the member must promptly pay over the entire amount to the client.

7. Members shall treat their clients' financial affairs as private and confidential, except for information customarily disclosed to interested parties as part of the process of placing rights as required by law, or, if agreed with the client, for other purposes.

8. The AAR believes that the practice of literary agents' charging clients or potential clients fees for reading and evaluating literary works (including outlines, proposals and partial or complete manuscripts) is subject to serious abuse that reflects adversely on our profession.

For this reason the AAR discourages that practice. New members and members who had not, before October 30, 1991, registered their intent to continue to charge reading fees shall not charge such fees. Effective January 1, 1996, all AAR members shall be prohibited from directly or indirectly charging such fees or receiving any financial benefit from the charging of such fees by any other party.

Until January 1, 1996, AAR members who, in accordance with the registration provisions of the previous paragraph, do charge such fees are required to comply with the following:

A. Before entering into any agreement whereby a fee is to be charged for reading and evaluating any work, the member must provide to the author a written statement that clearly sets forth: (i) the nature and extent of that report; (ii) whether the services are to be rendered by the member personally, and if not, a description of the professional background of the person who will render the services; (iii) the period of time within which the services will be rendered; (iv) under what circumstances, if any, the fee charged will be refunded to the author; (v) the amount of the fee, including any initial payment as well as any other payments that may be requested by the member for additional services, and how that fee was determined (e.g., hourly rate, length of work reviewed, length of report, or other measure; and (vi) that the rendering of such services shall not guarantee that the member will agree to represent the author or will render the work more saleable to publishers.

B. Any member who charges fees for such services and who seeks or facilitates the member's inclusion in any published listing of literary agents, shall, if the listing permits, indicate in that listing that the member charges such fees. Apart from such listings, members shall not solicit reading fee submissions.

C.   The rendering of such services for a fee shall not constitute more than an incidental part of the member's professional activity.

Appendix 4

The Parts of a Nonfiction Proposal

A nonfiction proposal usually ranges from thirty-five to seventy pages and includes the following:

I. The Introduction:
   The Overview, Resources Needed to Complete the Book, and About the Author sections enable you to provide as much ammunition about you and your book as you can muster.

   - Overview
     1. The subject hook—the most exciting, compelling thing that you can say that justifies the existence of your book: a quote, event, anecdote, statistic, idea, or joke. The book hook includes 2, 3, and 4 below.
     2. The title (and subtitle)
     3. The book's selling handle—a sentence that begins; [Title of book] "will be the first book to . . ."
     4. The length of the book (and number of illustrations), arrived at by estimating the backmatter and outlining the book
     5. The book's other special features: tone, humor, structure, anecdotes, checklists, exercises, sidebars, and anything you will do to give the text visual appeal
     6. The identification of a well-known authority who will give your book credibility and salability and has agreed to write a preface. If you can't get a commitment, write, "The author will contact A, B, and C for a preface."
     7. What you have done to answer technical or legal questions. If the book's on a specialized subject, name the

expert who reviewed it. If your book may present legal problems, name the literary attorney who vetted it.

8. Back Matter: Use comparable books as a guide.

9. Markets for the book: Start with the largest one.

10. Subsidiary rights potential: List the possibilities discussed in chapter 8.

11. Spin-offs: If your book can be a series or lends itself to sequels, mention the other books.

12. What you will do to promote the book. This is potentially the most important part of the proposal. Make this list as long and strong as you can. Best openers: "The author will match the publisher's consumer promotion budget up to $X." "When the book is published, the author will present seminars (or talks) in the following X cities: . . ." Follow this with a list of the major cities around the country that you will get yourself to, the number of events you will continue to do a year, and the number of copies you will sell a year at these events.

    You can impress agents and editors with your ability to hire the publicist you mention; list the parts of the press kit you will create and the media outlets to which you will send it; speak at trade and consumer conferences; list the trade and consumer print, broadcast, and electronic media in which, through your contacts, you will receive time and space; and list prominent people in the field who will provide cover quotes.

    Also guaranteed to impress will be tie-ins with business or nonprofits that will buy X copies of the book for their employees or customers; that will review, excerpt, or publish a story about the book in their publications; or that will sponsor a speaking tour. These ideas are not equally applicable to all kinds of nonfiction. However, the greater the continuing national impact you can create for your book, the better the editor, publisher, and deal you will get for it. For more on promotion, see chapter 15.

13. A list of books that will compete with and complement yours: the title, author, publisher, year, price. In one sentence, describe what each book does and fails to do. End

with a list of the ways your book will be different and better than the competition. A list of books on the same subject that don't compete with yours will prove the marketability of the subject.

On two separate pages, list:

- Resources Needed to Complete the Book
  List out-of-pocket expenses for $500 or more, such as travel, illustrations, permissions, or a preface, and a round figure for how much they will cost. End with this: "The manuscript will be completed X months after the receipt of the advance." If time is the only resource you need, add this sentence to the end of the Overview.

- About the Author
  Tell editors everything that you want them to know about you in descending order of relevance and importance. Include your media experience. If you have an audio- or videocassette of you in action, mention it. If you will meet with interested editors (at your expense), say so.

  If you have ideas for books that don't relate to the book that you are proposing, mention up to three of them. Write your bio in the third person to avoid a page full of *I*s. Use the first person only if you wish to convey your passion or sense of mission about the project.

  On a blank, unnumbered page after the bio, affix a 5-by-7 or 8-by-10 photograph that makes you look like a successful author and, if possible, relates to the book.

II. Chapter-by-Chapter Outline
The second part of the proposal must convince an editor that the idea will generate a book's worth of information and that you know the best structure to present it.

Start with a page listing the chapters and the page of the proposal on which each chapter outline begins. Chapter titles should, when appropriate, tell and sell.

For an A-to-Z reference book, the outline will be the list of entries. For a book with identically structured chapters—for example, a guidebook to ten great cities—just list the cities and what you will cover about each city in the section about the book's special features.

For most books, start each chapter outline on a new page, and aim for one line of outline for every page of text you guesstimate: for example, nineteen lines of outline for a nineteen-page chapter.

III. Sample Chapters
An article that is long enough and strong enough may substitute for a sample chapter. For a reference book, submit at least 10 percent of the text. For a guidebook to ten great cities, you only need one city. For a photography book, submit the introduction to the book, 20 percent of the prints and captions, and sheets of duplicate slides for as much of the book as you have. For a humor book, send at least 30 percent of the text. If it's a short book, send all of it.

For most books from new authors, editors would like the two strongest, representative chapters you can send, forty to fifty pages of sample material. If more chapters will create more enthusiasm for the book, send more.

For an inspirational story that reads like a novel and will have the greatest impact if the editor sees all of it, submit all of it with the Introduction and a short synopsis instead of an outline.

This list is adapted from but, alas, not a substitute for my book *How to Write a Book Proposal* (Cincinnati: Writer's Digest Books, 1985).

Appendix 5

Writers Organizations

American Society of Journalists & Authors, 1501 Broadway, Suite 302, New York, NY 10036; (212) 997-0947

Associated Writing Programs, George Mason University, Tallwood House, MS-1E3, Fairfax, VA 22030; (804) 683-683-3839

Austin Writers League, 1501 West Fifth Street, Suite E2, Austin TX 78703; (512) 499-8914

Authors Guild, 330 West 42nd Street, New York, NY 10036; (212) 563-5904

California Writers' Club, 2214 Derby Street, Berkeley, CA 94705

Editorial Freelancers Association (EFA), 71 West 23rd Street, New York, NY 10010; (212) 929-5400

Mystery Writers of America, 17 East 47th Street, Sixth Floor, New York, NY 10017

National Writers Association, 1450 South Havana, Suite 424, Aurora, CO 80012; (303) 751-7844

National Writers Union, 873 Broadway, Suite 2PW, New York, NY 10003; (212) 254-0279

PEN (Poets, Playwrights, Essayists, Novelists), American Center, 568 Broadway, New York, NY 10012; (212) 334-1660

PEN West, USA Center West, 672 South Lafayette Park Place, Suite 41, Los Angeles, CA 90057; (213) 365-8500

Poetry Society of America, 15 Gramercy Park West, New York, NY 10003; (212) 254-9628

Poets & Writers, 72 Spring Street, New York, NY 10012; (212) 226-3586

Romance Writers of America, 13700 Veterans Memorial Drive, Suite 315, Houston, TX 77014; (713) 440-6885

Science-Fiction & Fantasy Writers of America, 5 Winding Brook Drive, Suite 1-B, Guilderland, NY 12084

Western Writers of America, P.O. Box 823, Sheridan, WY 82801

Women's National Book Association, 160 Fifth Avenue, New York, NY 10010; (212) 675-7804

Writers Connection, P.O. Box 24770, San Jose, CA 95154; (408) 445-3600

For a comprehensive list, consult *Literary Market Place*.

Bibliography

Adams, Jane. *How to Sell What You Write*. New York: G.P. Putnam's Sons, 1984.

Adler, Bill. *Inside Publishing*. New York: Bobbs-Merrill, 1982.

American Society of Journalists and Authors. *The Complete Guide to Writing Non-Fiction*. Ed. Glen Evans. Cincinnati: Writer's Digest Books, 1983.

Appelbaum, Judith. *How to Get Happily Published: A Complete and Candid Guide*. 4th ed. New York: Harper Perennial, 1992.

Applebaum, Judith, and Florence Janovic. *The Writer's Workbook: A Full and Friendly Guide to Boosting Your Book's Sales*. Wainscott, NY: Pushcart Press, 1991.

Author Aid/Research Associates International, ed. and comp. *Literary Agents of North America: The Complete Guide to U.S. and Canadian Literary Agencies*. 5th ed. New York: Author Aid/Research Associates International, 1995.

Bail, Norman, ed. and comp. *The Writer's Legal and Business Guide*. New York: Arco Publishing, 1984.

Balkin, Richard. *How to Understand and Negotiate a Book Contract or Magazine Agreement*. Cincinnati: Writer's Digest Books, 1985.

Balkin, Richard. *A Writer's Guide to Book Publishing*. 3rd ed. Rev. Nick Bakalar and Richard Balkin. New York: Plume, 1994.

Begley, Adam, and Poets & Writers. *Literary Agents: A Writer's Guide*. New York: Penguin Press, 1993.

Bell, Herbert W. *How to Get Your Book Published: An Insider's Guide*. Cincinnati: Writer's Digest Books, 1985.

Bellkin, Gary S. *Getting Published: A Guide for Businesspeople and Other Professionals.* New York: John Wiley & Sons, 1984.

Bennett, Hal Zina, with Michael Larsen. *How to Write with a Collaborator.* Cincinnati: Writer's Digest Books, 1988.

Berg, A. Scott. *Max Perkins: Editor of Genius.* New York: Pocket Books, 1978.

Bernard, Andre. *Now All We Need is a Title: Famous Book Titles and How They Got That Way.* New York: Norton, 1994.

Bettmann, Otto L. *The Delights of Reading: Quotes, Notes and Anecdotes.* Boston: Godine, 1987.

Brinson, J. Dianne, and Mark F. Radcliffe. *The Multimedia Law Handbook.* Menlo Park, Calif.: Ladera Press, 1994.

Bunnin, Brad. *Author Law and Strategies: A Legal Guide for the Working Writer.* Berkeley, Calif.: Nolo Press, 1983.

Burack, A. S., ed. *The Writer's Handbook.* Boston: The Writer, 1993.

Burnham, Sophy. *For Writers Only.* New York: Ballantine, 1994.

Cassill, Kay. *The Complete Handbook for Freelance Writers.* Cincinnati: Writer's Digest Books, 1981.

Charlton, James, ed. *The Writer's Quotation Book: A Literary Companion.* Rev. ed. New York: Pushcart Press, 1985.

Charlton, James and Sam Gross, eds. *Books, Books, Books.* New York: Harper-Collins, 1988.

Charlton, James, and Lisbeth Mark. *The Writer's Home Companion.* New York: Franklin Watts, 1987.

Clark, Giles N. *Inside Book Publishing: A Career Builder's Guide.* London: Blueprint, 1988.

Cleaver, Diane. *The Literary Agent and the Writer: A Professional Guide.* Boston: The Writer, 1984.

Conrad, Barnaby. *The Complete Guide to Writing Fiction.* Cincinnati: Writer's Digest Books, 1990.

Copland, Lewis, and Faye Copland, eds. *10,000 Jokes, Toasts, and Stories.* Garden City, NY: Doubleday, 1965.

Corwin, Stanley J. *How to Become a Bestselling Author.* Cincinnati: Writer's Digest Books, 1984.

Coser, Lewis A., Charles Kadushin, and Walter W. Powell. *Books: The Culture and Commerce of Publishing*. New York: Basic Books, 1982.

Crawford, Tad. *The Writer's Legal Guide*. New York: Hawthorn Books, 1977.

Crawley, Tony, ed. and comp. *Chambers Film Quotes*. New York: W & R Chambers, 1991.

Curtis, Richard. *How to Be Your Own Literary Agent: The Business of Getting Your Book Published*. Exp. ed. Boston: Houghton Mifflin, 1983.

Davidson, Lance. *The Ultimate Reference Book: The Wit's Thesaurus*. New York: Avon, 1994.

Davis, Kenneth C. *Two Bit Culture: The Paperbacking of America*. Boston: Houghton Mifflin, 1984.

Delton, Judy. *The Twenty-Nine Most Common Writing Mistakes and How to Avoid Them*. Cincinnati: Writer's Digest Books, 1985.

Dessauer, John P. *Book Publishing: The Basic Introduction*, Exp. Ed. New York: Continuum, 1994.

Doran, George H. *Chronicles of Barabbas, 1884–1934*. New York: Harcourt, Brace, 1935.

Edelstein, Scott. *30 Steps to Becoming a Writer and Getting Published*. Cincinnati: Writer's Digest Books, 1993.

Editors of *Coda: Poets & Writers Newsletter*. *The Writing Business: A Poets & Writers Handbook*. New York: Pushcart Press, 1985.

Fife, Bruce. *An Insider's Guide to Getting Published*. Colorado Springs, Colo.: Piccadily Books, 1993.

Frank, Leonard Roy. *Influency Minds: A Reader in Quotations*. Portland: Feral House, 1995.

Frohbieter-Mueller, Jo. *Writing: Getting Into Print*. Lakewood, Colo.: Glenbridge, 1994.

Garvey, Mark. *Writer's Market*. Cincinnati: Writer's Digest Books, 1994.

Gee, Robin. *Novel and Short Story Writer's Market*. Cincinnati: Writer's Digest Books, 1995.

Glenn, Peggy. *Publicity for Books and Authors*. Huntington Beach: Aames Allen, 1985.

Goldin, Stephen and Kathleen Sky. *The Business of Being a Writer*. New York: Harper & Row, 1982.

Grannis, Chandler. *What Happens in Book Publishing.* New York: Columbia University Press, 1967.

Greenfield, Howard. *Books: From Writer to Reader.* New York: Crown, 1976.

Gross, Gerald, ed. *Editors on Editing: An Inside View of What Editors Really Do.* Rev. ed. New York: Harper & Row, 1985.

Gross, Gerald, ed. *Editors on Editing: What Writers Need to Know about What Editors Do.* 3rd ed. New York: Grove Press, 1993.

Healy. Lisa, ed. *My First Year in Book Publishing: Real-World Stories from America's Book Publishing Professionals.* New York: Walker, 1994.

Hendrickson, Robert. *The Literary Life and Other Curiosities.* San Diego: Harcourt Brace, 1994.

Hepburn, James G. *The Author's Empty Purse and the Rise of the Literary Agent.* London: Oxford University Press, 1968.

Herman, Jeff, and Deborah M. Adams. *Write the Perfect Book Proposal: 10 Proposals That Sold and Why.* New York: John Wiley & Sons, 1993.

Holm, Kirsten C. *Guide to Literary Agents.* Cincinnati: Writer's Digest Books, 1995.

Jackinson, Alex. *The Barnum-Cinderella World of Publishing.* New York: Impact, 1971.

Kirsch, Jonathan. *Kirsch's Handbook of Publishing Law.* Los Angeles: Acrobat, 1995.

Kozak, Ellen M. *From Pen to Print: The Secrets of Getting Published Successfully.* New York: Henry Holt, 1990.

Kozol, Jonathan. *Illiterate America.* New York: Anchor Press, 1985.

Kremer, John. *1001 Ways to Market Your Books.* Fairfield: Open Horizons, 1993.

Lakein, Alan. *How to Get Control of Your Time and Your Life.* New York: Signet Books, 1973.

Lamott, Anne. *Bird by Bird: Some Instructions on Writing and Life.* New York: Pantheon, 1994.

Larsen, Michael. *How to Write a Book Proposal.* Cincinnati: Writer's Digest Books, 1985.

Lazar, Irving. *Swifty: My Life & Good Times*. New York: Simon & Schuster, 1995.

Levine, Mark L. *Negotiating a Book Contract*. Wakefield, Mass.: Moyer Bell, 1994.

Levinson, Jay Conrad. *Earning Money Without a Job*. New York: Holt, Rinehart & Winston, 1979.

Levoy, Gregg. *This Business of Writing*. Cincinnati: Writer's Digest Books, 1992.

Lipsett, Suzanne. *Surviving a Writer's Life*. San Francisco: Harper San Francisco, 1994.

Literary Market Place: The Directory of American Book Publishing. New York: R. R. Bowker, 1985.

London, Jack. *Martin Eden*. New York: Airmont, 1970.

Lyon, Elizabeth. *Nonfiction Book Proposals Anybody Can Write: How to Get a Contract and an Advance before Writing Your Book*. Hillsboro, Oreg.: Blue Heron, 1995.

MacCampbell, Donald. *Don't Step on It–It Might Be a Writer*. Los Angeles: Sherbourne Press, 1972.

MacCampbell, Donald. *The Writing Business*. New York: Crown, 1978.

Mayer, Debby. *Literary Agents: A Writer's Guide*. New York: Pushcart Press, 1983.

McKenzie, Carole. *Quotable Sex*. New York: St. Martin's Press, 1992.

Meredith, Scott. *Writing to Sell*. 2nd ed. New York: Harper & Row, 1977.

Meyer, Carol. *The Writer's Survival Manual: The Complete Guide to Getting Your Book Published Right*. New York: Crown, 1982.

Miller, Peter. *Get Published! Get Produced! A Literary Agent's Tips on How to Sell Your Writing*. New York: Shapolsky, 1991.

Mogel, Leonard. *Making It in the Media Professions*. Chester, Conn.: Globe Pequot, 1988.

Mott, Frank Luther. *Golden Multitudes: The Story of Best Sellers in the United States*. New York: Macmillan, 1947.

Mungo, Ray. *The Learning Annex Guide to Getting Successfully Published.* New York: Citadel Press, 1992.

Naisbitt, John. *Global Paradox: The Bigger the World Economy, the More Powerful Its Smallest Players.* New York: Morrow, 1994.

Naisbitt, John. *Megatrends: Ten New Directions Transforming Our Lives.* New York: Warner Books, 1982.

Naisbitt, John and Patricia Aburdene. *Megatrends 2000: Ten New Directions for the 1990's.* New York: Morrow, 1990.

Nicholas, Ted. *How to Publish a Book and Sell a Million Copies.* Indian Shores: Enterprise-Dearborn, 1993.

Norwick, Kenneth P., and Jerry Simon Chasen. *The Rights of Authors, Artists, and Other Creative People: The Basic ACLU Guide to Author and Artist Rights.* 2nd. ed. Carbondale: Southern Illinois University Press, 1992.

Ohrbach, Barbara Milo. *All Things Are Possible: Pass the Word.* New York: Clarkson Potter, 1995.

Palmer, Florence K. *Confession Writer's Handbook.* Cincinnati: Writer's Digest Books, 19XX.

Pianka, Phyllis Taylor. *How to Get an Agent.* 1985.

Petersen, Clarence. *The Bantam Story: Thirty Years of Paperback Publishing.* New York: Bantam Books, 1970.

Peterson, Franklynn and Judi Kesselman-Turkel. *The Author's Handbook.* Englewood Cliffs, N.J.: Prentice-Hall, 1982.

Poets & Writers. *Into Print: Guides to the Writing Life.* New York: Quality Paperback Book Club, 1995.

Polking, Kirk, and Leonard S. Meranus, eds. *Law and the Writer.* Rev. ed. Cincinnati: Writer's Digest Books, 1981.

Polking, Kirk, Jean Chimsky, and Rose Adkins, eds. *Beginning Writer's Answer Book,* Rev. ed. Cincinnati: Writer's Digest Books, 1984.

Poynter, Dan. *The Self-Publishing Manual.* Santa Barbara, Calif.: Para Publishing, 1995.

Radcliffe, Mark. *Legal Issues in New Media.* Palo Alto, Calif.: Radcliffe, Ware & Freidenrich, 1995.

Reynolds, Paul R. *The Middle Man: The Adventures of a Literary Agent.* New York: William Morrow, 1972.

Reynolds, Paul R. *The Writing and Selling of Fiction*. Rev. ed. New York: William Morrow, 1980.

Ross, Tom and Marilyn Ross. *The Complete Guide to Self-Publishing*. Cincinnati: Writer's Digest Books, 1994.

Rovin, Jeff. *1001 Great Jokes*. New York: Signet, 1987.

Schiller, David. *The Little Zen Companion*. New York: Workman, 1994.

Seidman, Michael. *From Printout To Published*. New York: Carroll & Graf, 1988.

Shatzkin, Leonard. *In Cold Type: Overcoming the Book Crisis*. Boston: Houghton Mifflin, 1982.

Sheehan, Donald. *This Was Publishing: A Chronicle of the Book Trade in the Gilded Age*. Bloomington: Indiana University Press, 1952.

Strauss, Helen M. *Talent for Luck: An Autobiography*. New York: Random House, 1979.

Strunk, William, Jr., and E. B. White. *The Elements of Style*. 3rd ed. New York: Macmillan, 1979.

Swanson, H. N. *Sprinkled with Ruby Dust: A Literary and Hollywood Memoir*. New York: Warner, 1989.

Targ, William. *Indecent Pleasures*. New York: Macmillan, 1975.

Taylor, Phyllis. *How to Get An Agent*. Pianka, 1985.

Unwin, Sir Stanley. *The Truth about Publishing*. London: George Allen & Unwin, 1960.

Walters, Ray. *Paperback Talk*. Chicago: Academy Chicago, 1985.

White, John. *Rejection*. Reading, Mass.: Addison-Wesley, 1982.

Whiteside, Thomas. *The Blockbuster Complex: Conglomerates, Show Business, and Book Publishing*. Middletown, Conn.: Wesleyan University Press, 1981.

Wilbur, L. Ferry. *How to Write Books That Sell: A Guide to Cashing In on the Booming Book Business*. Chicago: Contemporary Books, 1979.

Zinsser, William. *On Writing Well*. 5th ed. New York: Harper Perennial, 1994.

Zuckerman, Albert. *Writing the Blockbuster Novel*. Cincinnati: Writer's Digest Books, 1994.

About the Author

Born and educated in New York City, Michael Larsen worked in promotion for three major publishers: William Morrow, Bantam, and Pyramid (now Jove). He and his wife, Elizabeth Pomada, moved to San Francisco in 1970. They started Michael Larsen/Elizabeth Pomada Literary Agents, Northern California's oldest literary agency, in 1972. Since then, the agency has sold books, mostly by new writers, to more than ninety publishers. Michael and Elizabeth are members of the Association of Authors' Representatives.

The agency represents book-length fiction and nonfiction for adults. Michael handles most of the agency's nonfiction; Elizabeth, most of the fiction.

Michael welcomes the opportunity to offer free consultations about nonfiction. The best time to call is after you have read his book *How to Write a Book Proposal*, so you understand what editors need, but before you start writing. Please call (415) 673-0939.

If you have completed a novel and tried it out on your professional network to make sure it's 100 percent, Elizabeth will be glad to see the first thirty pages and a synopsis. If you have had a novel published, please send the whole manuscript and a synopsis. Please include a self-addressed, stamped envelope with all correspondence, and allow up to eight weeks for the reading.

Michael and Elizabeth give talks on writing, agenting, and publishing. They also present workshops based on *How to Write a Book Proposal* and a seminar, "How to Make Yourself Irresistible to *Any* Agent or Publisher: The 100% Solution to Becoming a Successful Author," based on the material in this book, for universities, writers groups, and writers conferences.

With Hal Zina Bennett, Michael wrote *How to Work with a Collaborator*. He has reviewed books for the *San Francisco Chronicle*, and his articles have appeared in the *San Francisco Examiner*, *Writer's Connection*, *Writer's Digest*, and *Publishers Weekly*.

He conceived and collaborated with Elizabeth on California Publicity

Outlets (now Metro California Media) and the calendars and six books in the Painted Ladies series: *Painted Ladies: San Francisco's Resplendent Victorians; Daughters of Painted Ladies: America's Resplendent Victorians*, which *Publishers Weekly* selected as one of the best books of 1987; *The Painted Ladies Guide to Victorian California; How to Create Your Own Painted Lady: A Comprehensive Guide to Beautifying Your Victorian Home; The Painted Ladies Revisited: San Francisco's Resplendent Victorians Inside and Out*; and *America's Painted Ladies: The Ultimate Celebration of Our Victorians.*

For a free brochure about the agency, please send a #10 self-adressed, stamped envelope to 1029 Jones Street, San Francisco, CA 94109.